Discover the Power of
ONE

Discover the Power of
ONE

Make Your Life Count

Michael Youssef, PhD

New York   *Boston*   *Nashville*

FaithWords
Hachette Book Group USA
1271 Avenue of the Americas
New York, NY 10020

Visit our Web site at www.faithwords.com.

Designed by Paula Russell Szafranski

Printed in the United States of America

First Edition: November 2006
10 9 8 7 6 5 4 3 2 1

The FaithWords name and logo are trademarks of Hachette Book Group USA.

Library of Congress Cataloging-in-Publication Data

Youssef, Michael.
    Discover the power of one : make your life count / Michael Youssef.— 1st ed.
        p. cm.
    ISBN-13: 978-0-446-57953-7
    ISBN-10: 0-446-57953-X
    1. Self-actualization—Religious aspects—Christianity. 2. Christian life. I. Title.
    BV4598.2.Y68 2006
    248.4—dc22   2006006843

To Sarah Elizabeth, Natasha Ann,

Joshua David, and Jonathan Michael,

who have exercised the power of one.

Contents

Introduction

A Positive Presence in a Negative World

More than any other time in the history of Christendom, we need to teach our younger generation the vital importance of knowing how to unleash the power of one. Our very survival could depend on knowing and using the power of each single one.

I returned from an international preaching trip to find my home city in the grip of terror. An atmosphere of dread, suspicion, and fear filled the air.

On Friday, a man by the name of Brian Nichols had been taken to the new Justice Tower in downtown Atlanta to get ready for a retrial on rape charges and other violent felonies. As Nichols' handcuffs were removed so he might change from a jail jumpsuit into civilian clothes, he allegedly attacked his lone escort, critically injuring the sheriff's deputy. But that was only the beginning.

In a daylong rampage, Nichols allegedly shot five people, took and released hostages, and hijacked cars. He finally caught a commuter train to Lenox Square. There he apparently melted into the crowd of fans who were attending the Southeastern Conference men's basketball tournament in Atlanta.

Lenox Square is in Buckhead, the area of Atlanta where our church is located.

The trail was cold. Nobody knew where Nichols had gone. Virtually everybody believed he was hiding out someplace in the city. But who knew where he would appear next, or whom he might take hostage or kill? He was armed and deadly dangerous.

One person had caused a major metroplex to panic and experience meltdown. National crime statistics didn't matter at that point. All that mattered was finding one person in whom all criminal intent had taken root and produced a violent harvest of bloodshed and death.

A couple of hours after midnight, another person in Atlanta entered the story. Her name: Ashley Smith.

Although Smith had a troubled past, including some minor brushes with the law, she had recently committed her life to Jesus Christ and was seeking to grow in her relationship with the Lord. Her husband had been murdered several years before, and Smith was in the process of trying to get a new job in the greater Atlanta area so she could better provide for herself and her five-year-old daughter. She was unpacking in a new apartment when she decided to run an errand to a nearby convenience store. The time was 2 AM.

Smith noticed a man sitting in a Chevrolet pickup as she left the apartment but didn't think much about it. She was more concerned, however, when he was still sitting in the pickup after she returned from her errand. Moments later, she was taken hostage at gunpoint by Brian Nichols. He forced her into her apartment and tied her up with an extension cord.

They began to talk. Smith told Nichols about her husband's murder and explained that if he killed her, her little girl would have no mommy or daddy. She told him that her little girl was at her aunt's home and that she was scheduled to see her at ten o'clock the next morning at a church day-care center.

Through the nighttime hours, Smith began to gain the fugitive's trust. She asked Nichols if she could read to him and when he agreed, Smith picked up her Bible and an inspirational book. The conversation turned to God.

Nichols confessed to Smith that he had hurt some people and that he didn't want to hurt anybody else—he just wanted to rest in her home for a few days. He picked up photos of her family and, responding to this interest, Smith continued to talk to Nichols about her family and her faith. He admitted to her he was lost and that he felt God had led him to her. He eventually told her that he thought she was an angel sent from God.

Nichols asked her what she thought he should do. She said, "Turn yourself in. If you don't turn yourself in, lots more people are going to get hurt. And you're probably going to die." He watched a little television and saw a report of his own killing spree. He said to her, "I cannot believe that's me on there."

At about nine o'clock, Nichols asked Smith what time she had to leave to see her little girl. She told him she needed to leave at nine thirty and he agreed to let her go. He put the guns under the bed, handed her forty dollars, and said, "You might need this money. I don't need it. I'm going to be here for the next few days." He volunteered to hang pictures or put up curtains while she was gone.

Smith left her apartment complex in her car and immediately called 911. Shortly after ten o'clock that morning, a SWAT team arrived at the apartment. By noon, Nichols had been taken into custody without incident.

Not only was Ashley Smith highly praised for her courage and calm levelheaded thinking during her hours with Nichols, but the national media picked up her story and she had an opportunity to give witness to her faith before millions of television viewers in the days that followed. Her witness to Nichols had no doubt spared her life and Nichols' life. It also blessed the nation.

As part of an official statement she made to the press, Smith said: "As I'm sure you can imagine, this event has been extremely difficult and exhausting for me and my extended family. I have experienced just about every emotion one could imagine in the span of just a few days. Throughout my time with Mr. Nichols I continued to rely on my faith in God. God has helped me through tough times before and he will help me now. . . . Thank you again for your prayers. God bless you all" (*Atlanta Journal-Constitution,* March 4, 2005).

Can one person make a difference?

Yes!

The difference can be for bad—or for good.

The difference can impact just a few—or millions of people.

The difference can be practical, material, and for the day—or it can have eternal consequences.

Differences nearly always come down to one person's taking a positive initiative and becoming a positive presence in a negative situation.

Countless people had been speaking out about and conducting demonstrations in favor of civil rights in the 1960s, but it was one Christian woman, Rosa Parks, who triggered the real turnaround in the South. Her defiant act of sitting in the "whites only" section of a city bus was a one-woman stand against segregation. It was an act that started a much bigger cultural revolution.

Countless people were voicing their displeasure with government actions in China prior to one lone person standing before a tank in Tiananmen Square in Beijing. That one person's bravery was the incident the world remembers as a pivotal point in China's moving away from strict communist policies and isolationism.

The crumbling of communism in Eastern Europe had been occurring for decades, but it was the voice of one man—President Ronald Reagan—saying, "Mr. Gorbachev, tear down this wall" that resonated around the world. Within weeks, people, goods, ideas, and the gospel message were freely flowing between East and West Germany.

While these incidents are standout moments on the international stage, just as many quiet moments take place from day to day in apartment complexes, office buildings, social gatherings, and churches.

It's at the one-person level that change is initiated and propelled forward.

Jesus said about all forms of trial and trouble, "In the world you will have tribulation; but be of good cheer, I have overcome the world" (John 16:33 NKJV). Because Jesus overcame all evil, and because we as Christians live and move and have our being in Christ Jesus, the Lord challenges us to overcome the negative cultural pressures of this world just as He did! He tells us, "You *can* live a victorious life. You *can* make a difference. You *can* stand strong for the truth and know the blessings of a life God honors."

That's the central theme of this book. Even if you read no farther than this page, I trust you will walk away with the truth of God's Word: You *can* live an overcoming, positive life, even in the most negative and oppressive circumstances. You *can* be a positive presence in the face of negative pressure!

It starts with believing that you *can*, with God's help, make a difference for good and for God in your world, no matter how dark, pressure-packed, or troublesome that world may be.

Come discover for yourself the astounding power one can make in the world today. That one person can be you.

Discover the Power of
ONE

The Power of One Is Unlimited

Everywhere I look these days, I see teams: Sports teams. Management teams. Project teams.

In the church, we have team evangelism. In the retail world we have sales teams, and in schools we have team-taught courses and small group projects.

While teams can accomplish much, we must never overlook the fact that just one person taking a stand for what is right— and in turn, voicing and acting on what is right—can also accomplish much.

The power of one Christian is unlimited.

How can I say that with confidence?

Because God's Word tells us, through countless examples, that the power of one person is never limited to that person's

We may boldly say:
"The LORD is my helper:
I will not fear.
What can man do to me?"
(HEBREWS 13:6 NKJV)

abilities, intelligence, skills, or personality. A Christian is a person who is vitally linked to an unlimited God, regardless of the person's background, race, culture, IQ, social status, or job.

The connection with God comes by faith when a person accepts Jesus Christ as his or her personal Savior, acknowledging fully that Jesus was crucified on a cross to be the atoning sacrifice for that person's sins. When a person places his faith in Jesus, he experiences God's forgiveness. And since sin is what separates us from God, forgiveness, in turn, is what puts us back into right relationship with God. The Christian does not walk alone in this life. He or she walks in intimate relationship with God, who hung the stars in space and molded the mountains with His hands.

> You may be small. God is not.
> You may be weak. God is not.
> You may be limited. God is not.

Jesus described our relationship with God by saying, "I will pray the Father, and He will give you another Helper, that He may abide with you forever — the Spirit of truth, whom the world cannot receive, because it neither sees Him nor knows Him, but you know Him, for He dwells with you and will be in you. I will not leave you orphans; I will come to you" (John 14:16–18 NKJV).

What does this mean to us today?

An Awesome God Is on Your Side!

First, it means we are never alone. The Bible says that God is omnipresent, which means always present (2 Chron. 6:18; Eph. 4:6). He is not only eternal and everlasting, but He exists fully in every moment. He is with you right now, and in the minutes and hours to come. He is always accessible, twenty-four hours a day, seven days a week, every week of the year. The Bible says, "He Himself has said, 'I will never leave you nor forsake you'" (Heb. 13:5 NKJV).

Second, it means that the fullness of God's power and ability is available to us. God is:

- All-powerful. God is almighty—which means "all mighty." God can do *anything*. He not only created all things, but He sustains all things. He does what He wills to do, when He wills to act.
- All-wise. God knows everything about you and everything about your situation. He knows everything that is coming against you. He already knows the way through your problem, all the way to a victorious end. He already has made full provision for everything you need now and in your future.
- All-loving. The Bible says that God is love. Love is His very nature. Love is the underlying motive for all God does. Nothing, absolutely nothing, can separate you from God's love once you know Jesus as your Savior. The Bible says,

Who shall separate us from the love of Christ? Shall tribulation, or distress, or persecution, or famine, or nakedness, or peril, or sword? . . . In all these things we are more than conquerors through Him who loved us. For I am persuaded that neither death nor life, nor angels nor principalities nor powers, nor things present nor things to come, nor height nor depth, nor any other created thing, shall be able to separate us from the love of God which is in Christ Jesus our Lord. (Romans 8:35, 37–39 NKJV)

Third, to have God on your side means that God will help you overcome times of trouble. The Bible tells us plainly, "Do not be overcome by evil, but overcome evil with good" (Rom. 12:21 NKJV). God doesn't tell you to do something you cannot do! God tells you what you *can* do. He says:

You *can* overcome evil.

You *can* produce what is good.

You *can* make a difference.

You *can* stand up to the culture crunch you are facing.

As a Christian, you can be 100 percent confident today that an all-powerful, all-wise, all-loving God is with you no matter what, and His desire is to help you change the negative into a positive.

The challenge we face is to remind ourselves continually that God is with us and to call upon Him for guidance and help at all times and in all circumstances, not just when we are facing an emergency.

See Your Troubled Time As an Opportunity for You and God to Produce Good

Not long ago I saw a little postcard on the refrigerator door at a friend's house. It said: "Remember: God has something up His sleeve besides His everlasting arm."

How true that is! God has a plan and a purpose for the ages. That plan and purpose cover every detail and every minute of *your* life! For reasons you may not understand at the time—and may never understand in your lifetime—God allows difficult times of intense pressure and culture crunch in your life. Every person experiences good times and bad times in varying proportions. God has reasons for allowing difficulty that is beyond human comprehension.

The prophet Daniel in the Old Testament of the Bible was one of the bright, rising young stars of Israel whom King Nebuchadnezzar of Babylon ordered be taken captive. The giant wheels of Babylonian pressure and persecution had rolled over Jerusalem and left utter devastation in their wake. Daniel was suddenly and totally uprooted from his culture and transported to the land of Shinar—an alien place in which people worshiped alien gods.

Even in a position of captivity, however, Daniel experienced the fullness of God's purpose for his life. God had not forgotten Daniel.

God had not ceased to aid and assist Daniel. God did not need to shift from Plan A for Daniel's life to a Plan B. No! God's purpose for Daniel was that Daniel accomplish a great good in a negative world—to be a strong witness for God, and a strong encouragement to His people, in a heathen land.

God provided for Daniel in exile. The Bible tells us that God "brought Daniel into the favor and goodwill of the chief of the eunuchs" in the king's court (Dan. 1:9 NKJV).

God put Daniel into the king's most elite training program.

God arranged a relationship between Daniel and one of the king's most trusted aides.

God authorized "favor and goodwill" on Daniel's behalf.

Daniel is a superb role model when it comes to the power of one person to make a difference. It is his story—and his example—that is at the heart of this book. Daniel's impact and influence were far-reaching—indeed, his influence reaches all the way to you and me! Know this: what God did through Daniel, He can do through *you*. Open your mind and heart to believe it can happen!

A Purpose That Is for Eternal Good

Not only can you count on God's being with you in a time of trial, persecution, or strong temptation, but you can count on God's having a purpose for the difficult circumstances you are facing. His purposes are ultimately for *eternal good*.

This is a critically important point, and I don't want you to miss it.

Everything God does has a purpose. His purposes are not bound to the moment or to time as we know it. God's purposes are for eternity.

This means that everything God does on this earth—including all that He desires to do through your life—has the seed of eternal benefit in it. No matter what happens to you, if you will stand firm on God's principles and trust God to work in you, through you, and all around you, you can have 100 percent confidence that what you and God do together will have an *eternal* impact.

What good news this is!

It means that when you and God lock arms—your finite, frail, earthly arms linked with His everlasting and unlimited, all-powerful, all-embracing arms—you cannot fail. You *will* have an impact on your world. And you *will* have an impact on eternity.

Every act of kindness, every word of blessing, every strong stance you take for the truth, every righteous action you take, and every godly relationship you forge is something God can and will use to accomplish His eternal purposes—both in your life as an individual and in the lives of others around you.

Take heart!

You are never alone.

Your efforts to exert positive peer pressure on your world do not go unnoticed and do not fail to produce.

God is with you.

God is using you.

The true power and impact of your life is as unlimited as the God you love and in whom you trust.

Establishing Christ's Presence in Your World

Contact someone you know today who is as concerned about a negative situation or circumstance as you are. Share this chapter with that person—perhaps read it aloud to him or her, copy it and send it to the person, or buy the person a copy of this book. Ask the person to consider entering into an agreement with you that together, you will begin to trust God in new ways to work in you and through you to change this negative circumstance.

Reflect or Discuss

- In what ways do you recognize that you have not been trusting God to be big enough or to care enough about your particular problem or negative circumstance? How might you begin to trust God more?
- What might be some of the eternal purposes God has

in mind by putting you, His beloved child and trusted ally, in a position that seems filled with persecution or pressure?

You are connected to an *unlimited* God who specializes in possibilities and positives.

CHAPTER TWO

You Can Maintain Your Identity

Have you ever been called a name related to your appearance or personality?
Sometimes such names are derogatory
in nature, but sometimes names related
to a person's identity are positive. A person might be called "The Brain," "Mr.
Cool," "Quick-Draw," or "Diva."

Perhaps you were given a nickname
as a child that stuck well into your adult
years and it became an embarrassment.
I once heard of a man who was well
over six feet tall but his family members
still called him "Shorty." Another man
weighed nearly three hundred pounds
but friends from high school still called
him "Slats." A woman whose hair had
been gray for twenty years was called
"Red" by her husband because her hair

*I have raised you up for this
very purpose, that I might
show you my power and
that my name might be
proclaimed in all the earth.*
(EXODUS 9:16)

had been auburn in color when he had met her at age twenty-two.

Perhaps it is your last name that gives you away. When people hear my last name, Youssef, they know that I'm not from "these parts" of Atlanta where I have lived for thirty years. They don't even have to see my face or hear me speak to know that I'm not a good ol' boy from the South.

In the ancient world, a name was a person's identity. It was far more than a distinguishing label or an indicator of family heritage. A person's name said something about who the person was in character or nature.

Most babies in Bible times were not named until the eighth day after their birth. This gave parents a little time to note the characteristics of their child—not only the physical ones, but the traits in their personalities and gestures that might give an indication about the nature of the child. In addition, it was a custom in Bible times that mothers spent hours singing and talking to their unborn children, bonding with them in a deep emotional and spiritual way. This bonding gave mothers special insight into the personalities and destinies of the babies in their wombs.

Four young men in ancient Israel had names that revealed a great deal about them. When they were born in Jerusalem in the last part of the sixth century before Jesus Christ, these young men were given names that both revealed their identity and gave them their identity:

- Daniel's name meant "God has judged."
- Hananiah's name meant "Jehovah has been gracious."
- Mishael's name meant "Who is like God?"
- Azariah's name meant "Jehovah has helped."

Note that each of these four young men had a name that included something about the nature of God. From the book of Daniel, we know that Daniel was gifted in administration and was able to make excellent judgment calls throughout his lifetime.

It is no accident that his name in Hebrew meant "God has judged."

Hananiah knew the gracious nature of God. Mishael knew that there was nobody like God. Azariah knew that Jehovah was the One who helped him. These three men knew without any doubt that God's mercy and sovereign protection were behind the miracles they experienced all through their years in Babylon.

These four young men were just teenagers when Babylonian invaders took them by force from their families and from their homeland in 605 BC. Daniel was only fourteen years old and he was probably the oldest of the four.

God allowed Nebuchadnezzar to gain control over the land of Israel and to take captive the best and brightest of Israel's youth, along with the wealth of the nation. The captivity was prophesied to last seventy years but Daniel and his friends didn't know with certainty that they would be alive when the captivity was reversed. As far as they knew personally, this change in their lives was permanent.

Nebuchadnezzar was ruthless, but also smart. Talk about a brain drain! He took the cream of the crop to the city of Babylon, where he had these young men put into intense training, which we might call brainwashing. Nebuchadnezzar wanted to use these bright and handsome youths in his service to expand his power, but first, he had to make them usable. He had to change their identity from Jewish to Babylonian. To do this, he put his young captives through a training program designed to qualify them for positions of service. The program was like a three-year crash course at the college level.

Perhaps the ultimate attempt at changing the identity of these four young Hebrew men came about very quickly after their arrival in Babylon. The first order of Babylonian indoctrination was to change their names.

Daniel was given the name Belteshazzar, which means "keeper of the hidden treasure of Bel." Bel was the supreme Babylonian god—the name Bel was another name for Baal, a false god about which the Israelites knew a great deal because many of their enemies had worshiped this god.

Hananiah's name was changed to Shadrach, which was a name linked to the false god Merdoch.

Mishael's name was changed to Meshach, which is another name for the false god Venus.

Azariah's name was changed to Abednego, which meant "servant of Nego," yet another pagan god.

These four young men went from names that rooted their identity in Jehovah God to names rooted in the identity of pagan gods of Babylon.

The Babylonians may have changed the names of these young men, but these brave and confident young Hebrew teenagers refused to lose their identity in Jehovah. They continued to worship Jehovah and to rely upon Jehovah. Everything about their speech and behavior reflected their belief in Jehovah—which means, just as importantly, that nothing about their behavior reflected any reliance upon or identification with the pagan gods of Babylon.

What a critical lesson this is for us today!

Who Does God Say You Are?

What identity has God given to you? Who does God say you are? Does God call you a Christian? What other people say about you isn't important as long as you know God calls you a Christian! If God the Father says you are in right relationship with Him through your believing upon Jesus Christ and accepting the shed blood of Christ as the atonement for your sins, then you are a Christian! If God calls you His beloved child, then you are His beloved child.

God has a unique plan and purpose for your life. Nobody else can fulfill that part of His plan—only *you.* The power of one begins with your knowing and embracing the truth that you are irreplaceable. Your role is not to be like every person or to be like any one person. Your role is to be the *you* God created you to be. The power of one is all about your filling the place God has prepared uniquely for you.

Many people today, unfortunately, don't have full confidence about who God says they are. They simply don't know who they are according to the Bible. God's Word tells us that as people who have received Jesus Christ as our Savior, we are:

- Righteous, which means we are in "right standing" with God according to what Jesus has done, not because of what we have achieved, accomplished, or earned.
- Forgiven, with the slates of our pasts wiped clean so we might move forward in our lives, free to serve God and receive His blessings and rewards.
- Destined for eternal life, with heavenly homes already under construction on our behalf.
- Indwelled with the presence of the Holy Spirit, who is the Spirit of Truth leading us and guiding us into the right way to respond to all sorts of situations. It is the Holy Spirit who gives us the power to obey God's commandments and to live changed lives.
- Beloved. The Bible gives us a very long list of attributes that God has for His children, but perhaps the most important is *beloved.* We are God's cherished children, heirs with Christ Jesus of the fullness of God's kingdom.

If you don't know what God says about you, and if you do not draw your ultimate identity from who God says you are, you will be easily swayed—and then dismayed—by what other people or the world as a whole says about you.

The world will call you Goody Two-Shoes. God says you are pure and undefiled.

The world will call you a "wimp" for turning the other cheek when people persecute you. God says you are humble and strong.

The world will call you "stupid" for giving tithes and offerings to the work of God. God says you are in the best possible position for an abundant harvest of blessings.

The world will call you "weak" for needing a spiritual crutch. God calls you highly intelligent for recognizing that you are not all-powerful, all-knowing, or ever-present—and that God is.

The world will call you "crazy" for going to church on Sunday mornings instead of sleeping in or going to the lake. God calls you faithful.

The world will call you "intolerant" for calling some behavior right and other behavior wrong. God calls you wise for knowing right from wrong, and God calls you courageous for speaking up for what is right.

Don't trust the world to give you your identity. It will always give you an identity that is highly flawed and far short of your God-given potential.

At the same time the world criticizes you for following Christ, the world is likely to try to entice you with another set of words that are aimed at offering you an identity in keeping with the world's values:

- Successful
- Rich
- Famous
- Nice

Godly people can be successful. Godly people can be rich and famous. They certainly can and should be nice. But the ways in which the world uses these terms holds out the possibility that a person can be truly successful, genuinely rich, exceedingly famous, and extremely nice without God. That simply isn't possible.

It is God who allows people to rise to positions of prominence. It is God who gives people the ability and intelligence to make money and manage it well. It is God who allows our hearts to beat yet another beat, and for the lungs to draw yet another breath so that we can live and work yet another day. It is God who gives a person a true ability to forgive, to love, to reflect pure joy, to be patient, and to live a life that is under control. It is God who gives a person the ability to be merciful to those who don't deserve any mercy, to tolerate sinners while not tolerating sin, and to be generous toward people who don't deserve generosity.

The world's definitions for *successful, rich, famous,* and *nice* are limited only to the finite nature of mankind. Since man is fickle, times change, and any degree of accomplishment is always fleeting, the world's definitions are always subject to revision. God's definitions for us are sure and lasting. They do not change because God does not change. What He says about us has eternity written all over it!

Jesus Gave Us His Name

In giving us His name, Jesus gave us His identity. The word *Christian* means "little Christ" or "like Christ." The word *Christian* refers to a person who is so like Christ that if people didn't know when Jesus lived in history and had only heard about His nature and character, they would think Jesus was speaking or acting when you show up to speak or act. As Christians, our words and actions are to mirror what Jesus did and to embody what Jesus would do if He suddenly was walking in our shoes in our world.

As a Christian, you find your supreme identity in that word *Christian*. You are not Joe or Betty or Bill or Jessica who is a good person. You are a Christian who happens to be known by people as Joe, Betty, Bill, or Jessica. Christian is a noun — it is your identity. It is your supreme name.

Jesus said to His followers, "You may ask me for anything in my name, and I will do it" (John 14:14). He gave His followers the authority to heal the sick and cast out demons in His name. He gave them the ability to solve problems and meet needs in His name. It is because Jesus has given us His name — His full identity — that we have the power and authority to stand confidently in the midst of a sinful world and say, "I am choosing this day whom I will serve, and the One I choose to serve is Jesus Christ."

Establishing Christ's Presence in Your World

As you prepare to go out into the world today — perhaps to a place of employment, a place of ministry, or to a meeting with a friend or acquaintance — say to yourself, *I am going out this door into the world in the name of Jesus. What I do in the coming hours I am doing in the identity of Jesus, just as if Jesus were wearing these clothes and walking in these shoes and going where I am about to go to en-counter the people I'm about to meet.* Then, walk in the identity of Jesus all through your day. Say what you know Jesus would say. Do what you know Jesus would do. Take on His identity.

Encourage others around you who are Christians not to give in to what the world may say about them. Instead, speak to your Christian friends what you know to be their identity in Christ.

Reflect or Discuss

- What has someone who is in the world—perhaps an ungodly boss or coworker or neighbor—said about you? How does that person define you? What names does he or she call you? What does God's Word say?
- How difficult is it to stay reminded of who God says we are? What specific challenges do you face when it comes to standing tall for Christ in the face of ridicule or rejection?
- What are the challenges facing a person who has never known what God says about him but rather has heard words of criticism or false identity all his life?
- What might a person do to adopt a new identity that is totally in line with God's Word?

God has given you His name so that you might reflect the fullness of His identity and character *today*.

CHAPTER THREE

You Can Challenge the Status Quo

Daniel and his friends—Hananiah, Mishael, and Azariah—were thrust almost overnight into a world in which they did not have any status and didn't really understand the status quo.

Have you ever been in such an environment? Perhaps you were traveling in another nation or in a part of the United States where the customs were very different. Suddenly you were a nobody, a stranger. You didn't know the "rules" of the new place, or how to behave appropriately. You felt scared, or at the very least, nervous that you were about to do something offensive or embarrassing. The first thing you likely did was sit back, try to become invisible, and observe the behavior of others so you might better fit in.

What do righteousness and wickedness have in common? Or what fellowship can light have with darkness? What harmony is there between Christ and Belial? What does a believer have in common with an unbeliever? What agreement is there between the temple of God and idols?

(2 CORINTHIANS 6:14–16)

I certainly felt that way when I moved from the Middle East to Australia. I was twenty years old. No world could have been more foreign to me! My accent gave me away at every turn. My familiarity with the English language wasn't at all what it is today. My understanding of the customs was better described as "no understanding." I felt adrift. Had I not been in the company of Christians who at least believed in the same God and knew the same Bible, I would have been overwhelmed. I spent many hours watching and listening to the people around me in order to learn how better to fit in to this new culture in which I was determined to study for several years.

Living in a Foreign Land

Daniel and his friends very likely also sat back and observed the world in which they found themselves—but not for long. No doubt the trek from Jerusalem to Babylon had taught them a number of things with great certainty.

Daniel and his friends knew, for example, that Babylon was a foreign land. How important it is to know that the land in which you live is not your eternal home or destiny. The Bible clearly tells us that heaven is our home and we are just passing through this earth (1 Pet. 1:17).

We also need to recognize that the United States is a foreign land to many native-born citizens! The sad truth is that Christians today are living in a land that most assuredly would be foreign to their parents or grandparents. The United States is simply no longer a Christian nation. Certainly the founding fathers of the United States were mostly Christians and the principles embedded in the Constitution and other statements made at the formation of the United States are strongly Christian in nature. Every state's constitution has markings of divine destiny and reliance upon God. What do I mean, then, when I say that the United States is no longer a Christian nation?

The majority of people in our nation today do not live devout

Christian lives. They may call themselves Christian, but they don't live out Christian values. They don't demand that their leaders be avowed Christians. They don't demand that the laws of the land be in accordance with Bible principles of truth and justice. They don't apply their Christian beliefs to their jobs or insist that the curriculum being taught to children in the public schools honors God as Creator and the Giver of important absolute commandments about human behavior, especially the Ten Commandments.

We live in a land that allows several hundred thousand unborn babies a year to be killed for the convenience of the parents who didn't mind getting pregnant but don't want a child—even as we say we value life.

We live in a land that is rampant with crime of all types, fueled by media programs that are filled with violent images and sexual innuendo—even though we may say we are against crime and sexual impurity.

We live in a land that allows widespread pornography—even as we decry the abuse of women and children.

We live in a land where the only sin that remains is the sin of intolerance. We claim to be loving and kind, but our "tolerant" attitude in reality allows sinners to keep sinning solely because that's what the sinners want to do, regardless of the very unkind and unloving consequences to those who don't want any experience with sin or its consequences. Sin always divides. It always produces decay of some type. It always claims innocent victims.

No, we do not live in a nation that lives the way Jesus lived, and that's what it means to be a Christian. We live in a foreign land that has emerged on our own soil.

Why the Captivity?

We are wise to understand just why Daniel and his friends found themselves in Babylon. Israel as a nation had turned a deaf ear to the Word of God and had refused repeatedly the warnings of the prophet Jeremiah. God's patience with His people had run out.

God allowed King Nebuchadnezzar from the neighboring empire of Babylon to invade Israel and put Jerusalem under siege. The Bible tells us that the Lord gave Jehoiakim king of Judah into his hand (Dan. 1:1–2).

How could God do this? Because there is a balance between God's mercy and God's justice. God will not tolerate ongoing rebellion. He puts a limit on our willful ignoring or disobeying His commandments. He allows enemies to strike at us and sometimes to take us captive, not out of anger or hatred, but rather as a chastisement so that we might come to our senses and return to Him. God chastises us to warn us and help us realize that we are wiser to obey than to disobey, that we must obey God if we are to have God's blessing, and that we must acknowledge our dependence upon Him if we are to live in right relationship with Him.

There's something that God wants us to learn as His children about the world in which we find ourselves. Discover what He is trying to teach you!

There's also something God wants us to do in response to those who are exerting authority over us. Learn from Daniel and his friends!

Take a Long Look at the World in Which You Find Yourself

Daniel and his friends were exceptionally bright and astute young men. I have no doubt at all that they were keenly observant and astute when it came to evaluating Babylon and the king's palace to which they were taken.

Daniel and his friends knew they had been taken by force. They had been ripped violently away from everything they knew: their families, their culture, their neighborhood, their city, their school, their marketplace, their normal foods and beverages, their music, their celebrations and festivals, their language, and their temple. They had been forced to travel hundreds of miles, on foot, to a place where they didn't know very many people, didn't speak the language, didn't know the customs, didn't know their way around, and didn't understand the beliefs and religion of the people who had taken them captive.

Talk about a shock to the system!

Talk about finding yourself in a confusing environment! Talk about feeling overwhelmed at every turn!

A young woman said to me not long ago, "I tried to imagine my great-grandmother sitting next to me on the sofa watching television last night. I could almost feel the embarrassment she would have felt. The commercials alone would probably have caused her to blush. Much of what she probably wouldn't have understood had to do with terms that are now euphemisms for sex. She would have been shocked. What was sad to me is that I'm not shocked at what would have shocked my great-grandmother. I'm so used to it that I don't even feel repulsed. That's not good!"

She's right. It's not good.

People today walk about as if they are in a dream, not even thinking the dream is a nightmare. Daniel and his friends were acutely aware that they were in a nightmare. Nothing they considered to be a reliable touchstone remained for them.

At the same time, they found themselves in the lap of luxury in Babylon. They were living in the invading king's palace, surrounded by pleasures and enticements. As violent as their captivity had been, they had landed in a soft and cushy place. As dismayed and unsettled as they must have felt, these young captive men must also have felt a certain degree of curiosity and wonder and awe at what they saw. So lavish the gold vessels and utensils! So fine the fabrics and carpets! So beautiful the buildings and gardens! As hard as their trek to Babylon had been and as different as this new place was, there was also the lure of pleasure in the king's palace. The world they now faced was drastically different . . . but was it all that bad?

Isn't that the same dilemma we face? The world in which we live is established on false beliefs and anti-Christian values, but it's a materially excellent world. Can such a luxurious world be so bad? Can things that make you feel so good be wrong?

Just as Daniel and his friends eventually concluded, we must conclude that the pleasure and opulence of the world are a façade. The environment underneath the surface enticements is an environment that is hostile to Christ, not just indifferent to Christ. Although the world demands tolerance *from* Christians, the world isn't tolerant *of* Christians! The world insists that Christians become less judgmental, less righteous, less of their faith and their relationship with God, less certain of their evaluations of right and wrong. The pressure is often intense to become less Christian—never is the pressure of the world to become more pure, more faithful, or more moral.

The glitz and glamour and bright lights of the world might blind a person temporarily. The offer of pleasure may seem genuine and overpowering at times. But underneath is the seamy side of sin. It is a side the devil never shows right away—the side that leads to decay, destruction, and death. Sin doesn't reveal its hard edge initially, but that edge is always there. In Babylon, things may have appeared pleasurable and pleasant for the young captives, but underneath the surface was evil intent.

Openly Recognize That You Are
Called to Be Different from the World

God does not desire that you be like the world at large. He presents in His Word a distinctly different and superior life than any life the world can offer. You are not like the ungodly people around you. Face that fact. Be kind and merciful to the ungodly. Do good to them and speak truth to them. But don't seek to become like them.

Daniel and his three friends never lost full recognition that the men who had control over them were their enemies, not their friends. They were in exile and in servitude, not on a pleasure cruise. They were captives, not tourists. This was no foreign-exchange trip for a group of high school students. Daniel and his friends' captors hated the young men and intended to use them; should they be found unusable, their captors would abuse them. Use and abuse—that's a tactic the devil has used for millennia. These four young men found themselves in a wicked world, with temptations to do evil rising up at every turn, every hour.

What Is It You Are Being Taught— and Required to Learn

A man said to me recently, "I have a coworker who automatically assumes that I believe what he believes about God. He automatically assumes that we belong to the same political party and want the same things from our government officials. He is 100 percent wrong, but I've discovered something important about myself. He believes these things because I haven't said anything to challenge him! He is trying to influence me, but I'm not influencing him!"

"What do you think would happen if you spoke up in response to what he says, or if you stated your beliefs first?" I asked.

"He'd probably think I'm weird," he said. "He'd probably tell others in the office that I'm a conservative whacko or he'd make snide little comments and critical facial gestures."

"And what would you do then?" I asked.

"I never really thought about it," he said. "I suppose I could ask him why he assumed that he's right and I'm so wrong. I suppose I could ask him why he thinks his opinion is the only one a person should have."

Right! We are called as Christians to challenge what other people hold as the status quo and the "politically correct" belief. We are called as Christians to challenge any opinion or belief that does not exalt the Lord!

Rather than roll over and play dead when others criticize you for believing in God and advocating a godly way of living, rise up and say, "What's so good about what you as a non-Christian believe? What I believe leads to a life of inner peace, purpose, joy, and satisfaction. What I believe leads to a life that has great potential for genuine fulfillment, forgiveness, and eternal life. What's so good about what you believe?"

Daniel and his friends definitely challenged the status quo in their world, even though they could do nothing to reverse their immediate captivity. They did not go along with everything that their captors initially demanded of them.

Where did the glamour of the palace and the guillotine of sin collide? In the curriculum of what these young Hebrew men were being taught—in other words, in the subject matter they were being required to learn. The Bible tells us that these young men had been chosen because they were smart. They would have scored sixteen hundred on the SAT and 150 on an IQ test. They were "gifted in all wisdom, possessing knowledge and quick to understand." Their Babylonian captors saw them as young men to "whom they might teach the language and literature of the Chaldeans" (Dan. 1:4 NKJV).

What was this language and literature of the Chaldeans? The Chaldeans were not Babylonians per se. They were men from a region, Chaldea, that the Babylonians had conquered. The Chaldeans had a long-standing reputation for being "spiritual." They could do magic tricks. They told stories that had veiled spiritual meanings. They adopted an air that they were more spiritual than the Babylonians, and they agreed to help the Babylonian rulers in exchange for safety and status.

The Babylonians, not at all sure about whether the Chaldeans were telling truth or lies, went along with them just in case the Chaldeans might be right. The Chaldeans were the power behind the throne, the spiritual gurus who influenced the emperor and other rulers of the land.

The literature of the Chaldeans told about the power of false gods. It was the language and literature of the fantastic, the so-called supernatural, the realm of gods and goddesses and their powers. It gave instructions in potions and rituals, mostly in the form of stories and fables. Daniel and his friends were being fed a pack of lies that were rooted in the very foundation of education:

- What is ultimately true?
- What is reliable and can be replicated?
- What is the meaning of life?
- What are the rules for success and reward?

If ungodly people are allowed to set the agenda for education, they will always present a world in which truth is relative and discernible by only a select few who have insider information or the power to evaluate correctly.

They will present a world in which nothing is truly reliable or lasting—everything is in flux or subject to editing according to "current standards." The past should not be replicated, for the most part, because it isn't cutting-edge. This means, of course, that the traditions of the past must give way to the whims of the present.

They will present a world in which the meaning of life is subject to redefinition and the rules for living a successful life are presented in terms of what a person can acquire or accomplish in his own strength or knowledge—never with the genuine help of God.

How is this different from a godly agenda for learning? A godly person presents a world in which truth is absolute and can be known by understanding the principles of God's Word. A godly person advocates a world in which God does not change, and neither does human nature. God's laws are absolute and lasting. In the curriculum of the godly, man is a sinner in need of redemption. God offers forgiveness.

What about the meaning of life? The meaning of life to the godly is founded upon the principles of worshiping God and obeying His commandments, then following His directives about loving and caring for one another. Success in life is defined as living a life that is marked by God's peace, a strong sense of purpose that one realizes fully only by helping others, and an expectation of eternal rewards from a loving God.

The Chaldeans taught in a way that was ultimately all about them. They claimed to serve the Babylonians when in truth, the Babylonians were giving them privileged access to the wealth and power of the land. How true this is in our world today! The ungodly who are governing the agenda of what our culture teaches us, which is far more extensive than what our school systems are teaching our children, are in search of personal power and wealth. They may claim that they are acting in the best interests of the underdogs and downtrodden, but in truth, the message they present keeps people in bondage to sin and to a host of other binding chains: low self-worth, lack of skills, and poverty. They claim to be advocates for freedom, but in truth, they leave people in a world that is anything but free.

There's no such thing as "free sex"—such a world results in rampant disease, unwanted babies, abortions, and neglected children, not to mention broken homes, a lack of responsibility among fathers, and tremendous disillusionment about the meaning of love. There's no freedom in any of that!

There's no such thing as a world in which every person can "do as he pleases." A world that operates by that principle is a world that is filled with crime, greed, and a savage competitive spirit that disregards and uses people at every turn.

There's no such thing as "no shame, no blame." Such a world creates people with callous hearts who care very little about the ways in which they hurt others.

There's no such thing as a world in which "everybody is equal." There are always going to be people who are smarter, richer, more talented, more athletic, and so forth—just as there are always going to be people who are "lesser than." This has nothing to do with equality before God or equality in the way justice is administered. The world's message says everybody should have a right to certain material goods, a right to take what a person wants, and a right to be taken care of until death. That's not possible, and an effort to achieve this promotes only jealousy and greed, not values related to work and responsibility.

Daniel and his friends knew from what they were being taught that they were in a strange land with a different set of values and status quo. They may have passed their courses, but they didn't buy the message.

They never lost sight that their teachers were ungodly men. They never lost sight of the fact that the spirituality being presented to them was rooted in evil. They never lost sight that they were being fed a message that denounced the glory of God.

We are wise to follow the example of these courageous young Hebrew men. We may learn the facts of history, science, geography, and language. We may be aware of the literature that is consumed by the masses. But we must open our eyes at all times to the real message that is being taught to us by ungodly people who are the creators and sustainers of an ungodly culture.

What is presented by the world as "spirituality" is not holy spirituality.

What is being presented by the world as "truth" is man's truth, not God's truth.

What is being presented by the world as "effective" and "productive" is not eternally effective or productive.

Daniel, through the power of one, influenced his friends. Together they didn't internalize or adopt the values or worldview that the Babylonians were foisting upon them. We must not adopt the values or worldview that the ungodly teachers of our age are presenting. If we do, we will never see the reason for discovering the power of one — and we will fail to seize the opportunities before us.

Establishing Christ's Presence in Your World

Question ungodly people who make statements that automatically assume you are in agreement with them. Ask very politely but directly, "Why do you believe that? On what basis? For what purpose?" If people begin to call you a name — usually because they have run out of logical answers to your questions — challenge what they are doing. Point out that you have not called them names, you have just asked questions!

Know what you believe and why. Get into God's Word and

study it. Find out what God really requires of those He calls His beloved children.

Reflect or Discuss

- Carefully evaluate just one night of prime-time television. What are the values it presents? How are they different from the values God's Word presents? Or tape and listen to a Sunday morning commentary program. What values underlie the editorial statements being made? Are the values in line with biblical values?
- What have others you admire done to challenge the status quo? In what ways were they effective? What can you learn from them?

Having status is not nearly as important as knowing the status quo. When the status quo is not in keeping with God's Word, challenge it.

CHAPTER FOUR

You Can Experience God's Rewards

I have never met a college student who truly liked dorm food, at least not after the first couple of weeks. Those who were studying in the college of King Nebuchadnezzar, however, likely loved the foods they were being given on a regular basis.

Make no mistake about it. Nebuchadnezzar had established a rigorous degree program for his captives from various nations. The three-year course of indoctrination included a heavy study schedule. The captives were receiving courses in mathematics, science, literature, geography, political science and protocol, and Babylonian history. They were learning the rituals, ceremonies, and beliefs of the Chaldeans. They were also expected to remain in top athletic form, strong and

Without faith it is impossible to please God, because anyone who comes to him must believe that he exists and that he rewards those who earnestly seek him.

(HEBREWS 11:6)

healthy so they might not only have the mental prowess but the physical stature associated with leadership in the Babylonian culture. The main bribe that kept these captives from rebelling against the heavy demands placed upon them were the luxuries they received in the king's palace.

Like athletes in American colleges today who often enjoy a menu that is not typical of that given to other students—an eating program with more protein and foods intended to help them build strong muscles and have great energy—these young captives in Babylon received a diet that was far from typical. The Babylonians were teaching them how to eat and drink like governors, not commoners.

Unfortunately, the foods of the governors of Babylon included many that were not in keeping with the dietary laws God had given to the Israelites. The Babylonian cafeteria was not kosher!

No doubt Daniel and the three who were impacted by him were impressed with the vast amount of food and types of food being set before them. They knew this food was a part of their being given privileged status in this new land. They knew that to a great extent, this life of luxury was meant as a bribe to get them to cooperate with their captors. Most of those who were in Nebuchadnezzar's training program were only too willing to cooperate in order to keep from being relegated to physical slavery or a life of severe hardship. The pressure to conform was intense, and the rewards for conforming were enticing. These young captives found themselves in an environment in which it was much easier to say yes than to say no.

The young captives also knew they had been chosen for this training in the king's court because they were smart, talented, and healthy. It didn't hurt that they were handsome too! The Bible tells us that these were "young men in whom there was no blemish, but good-looking, gifted in all wisdom, possessing knowledge and quick to understand, who had ability to serve in the king's palace" (Dan. 1:4 NKJV). It's very appealing for a person to believe he or she has been singled out for an honor on the basis of personal attributes.

Those who are chosen begin to act accordingly—they seek to live up to the honor bestowed on them.

Talk about pressure! These guys knew they were the select few.

These young men knew they were honored, set apart for privilege, and given an opportunity painted in terms of luxury. It would be easy to say:

- "Why not cooperate? They just want me to be prepared to lead."
- "Why not do everything they ask, when obeying is easy and disobeying could be deadly?"
- "Why not be Babylonian? After all, the Babylonians are ruling the world as we know it."
- "Why not take on a new identity? The old one got us captured and exiled, and what's so good about that?"

Aren't these the same things we are tempted to say in response to the pressures of our culture today? All around me I encounter people who say,

- "Why not see these movies and read these books and attend these events? You need to be part of your culture and know what's current."
- "Why not go along with the crowd? You won't be the success you want to be if you buck the tide."
- "Why not play the game of the power structure? You can't rise to the top of the corporate or political world unless you know how to play the game and play it well."
- "Why not be perceived as cutting-edge? Those who lag behind get left behind."

The answer is very simple: because God said that being "of the world" isn't the identity He desires for His people. He calls His people to a different standard. He gives His people a different identity. He challenges His people to change the world, not be changed by the world. Jesus prayed this for His followers: "They are not of the world any more than I am of the world. My prayer is not that you take them out of the world but that you protect them from the evil one. They are not of the world, even as I am not of it" (John 17:14–16).

You Don't Need to Do Things the Way the World Does Them

You *can* do things differently, with no less quality or effectiveness! You *can* win the world to your way of acting and behaving!

The Bible tells us that Daniel "purposed in his heart" that he would say "No, thank you" to the foods that were being offered to him (Dan. 1:8 NKJV). He decided to take action and seek a change in the "rules" regarding their treatment. He bucked authority in a way that was highly effective and in a way we are wise to copy:

- Daniel was polite. He said, "Please test your servants for ten days" (Dan. 1:12). He didn't demand. He asked.
- Daniel offered an alternative with a time limit. He came with a plan, not with a stubborn, rebellious attitude that would have conveyed, "I don't want to do things your way. It's a lousy way but I can't come up with anything better." He said to those in authority, "Please test your servants for ten days: Give us nothing but vegetables to eat and water to drink" (v. 12).
- Daniel was willing to leave the final analysis of the test to the captors. He said, "Compare our appearance with that of the young men who eat the royal food, and treat your servants in accordance with what you see" (v. 13).

If you don't like the ungodly practices in your workplace or community, go to those in leadership as Daniel did! Politely ask for a test of a "better plan." Put a time limit on the test and let it be known that you are willing for those in authority to evaluate the results objectively.

Note, too, that this plan Daniel offered didn't bring up theological issues. The plan dealt strictly with observable facts and behavior.

In truth, the foods the Babylonians offered to Daniel and his friends were wrong for them to eat not only because the delicacies likely included shellfish, fatty meats, and the meat of unclean animals. These delicacies were so called because the food had been offered first to the idols of the Babylonian pagan gods! The pagan peoples of the ancient world ate the leftovers of foods sacrificed to their gods as a means of identifying with the gods. They believed that if they ate the same food as the gods, they were worshiping and identifying with the gods, and the net result would be that the pagan gods would give them more power and less angst in their lives. The table of Nebuchadnezzar has serious overtones of worship ritual! Daniel, Hananiah, Mishael, and Azariah were being asked to eat the food of the gods as a form of worship of those gods.

Daniel refused. But in dealing with his enemy captors he didn't bring up the religious issues. He brought up the practical issues of eating alternate foods. And as you might suspect, the pagan gods of the Babylonians didn't have much delight in vegetables and water. There simply wasn't enough fat and sugar and alcohol in those foods to give "pleasure."

So, Daniel opted for what was in keeping with the dietary laws God had given, and for what was in keeping with the worship of God and not pagan idols. His captors likely never knew the real agenda behind Daniel's request.

As Christians we must never cover up or purposefully hide what we believe if we are asked. At the same time, we do not need to tell every purpose we have as we seek to change the culture in which we find ourselves. We should address needs from a practical standpoint, not from an argumentative theological standpoint. When the better idea that we offer works and produces a good result, people will be much quicker to hear the reasoning behind the plan!

At all times, we must treat the ungodly with respect as individuals so the Holy Spirit might have an even greater opportunity to

speak to their hearts about Christ Jesus. In many ways, Daniel offered a different plan with no lowering of standards. Daniel and
those who had been influenced by him agreed that their captors
could evaluate their appearance. They weren't asking for more
from their captors. They were actually asking for less—after all,
vegetables were cheaper, and certainly the rich foods that Daniel
and his friends didn't eat became bigger portions for those in immediate rule over them. By asking for something reasonable that
stood to benefit the captors, Daniel began to prevail and to earn the
respect of those over him.

If we are going to change our culture for Christ, we need to be
creative in the alternate plans we propose!

Don't Accept a Different World as Being an Unchangeable World

Above all else, Daniel did not accept the notion that the new world
in which he found himself was unchangeable. So many people today
say with a shrug of their shoulders, "Things aren't the way they used
to be. It's a different world!" True—the world isn't the way it used to
be fifty years ago. Some technology has changed. Communication
methods have changed. Prevailing cultural forces have shifted. But
overall, the heart of man has not changed from the beginning. Godly
people have faced evil and temptations for thousands of years. If
Daniel could face the full hurricane force of the Babylonian culture—
which was definitely a category five on the hurricane or tornado scales
of wind force—we can certainly face the storms that are assaulting
our world.

"The pressure is so intense," you may say as you feel tempted day
in and day out to join those around you in un-Christlike activities
or conversations. Don't be swayed by the pressure to join in. See
that pressure as a force that can make you stronger, not a force that
is about to do you in.

It's easy to be a Christian if you are standing in a stadium with
fifty thousand other believers. It's easy to be bold for Christ if you

are singing praises while you are surrounded by others who are singing with you in like-minded unity.

What truly defines you as a Christian is if you are able to swim against the tide of a raging river of hedonism. What reveals who you really are is how you behave when you are in a group of rowdy nonbelievers who are taunting you and tempting you to do what you know is contrary to God's commandments.

God honors and recognizes those who will stand up for the truth and speak up for Him. Jesus said, "Whoever acknowledges me before men, I will also acknowledge him before my Father in heaven. But whoever disowns me before men, I will disown him before my Father in heaven" (Matt. 10:32–33).

God rewards those who speak the truth in the face of error.

God rewards those who choose to live in a godly way in the midst of an ungodly culture.

God rewards those who trust in Him and display spiritual integrity.

Let me show how He did this with Daniel and his three friends by giving them "knowledge and understanding." He honored Daniel's leadership by giving him an ability to "understand visions and dreams of all kinds" (Dan. 1:17). These rewards from God made all the difference in the lives of these four men—the rewards ensured them positions of leadership and ultimately their lives.

There is no substitute for spiritual integrity. True spiritual integrity does not need a spiritual greenhouse for growth and maturity. Spiritual integrity becomes strong and mature when it is exposed to the most violent elements of sin, persecution, ridicule, yet stays strong in those environments.

Don't give in to excuses.

With God, you have all the "odds" you need to stand against the odds.

With God, you can withstand the forces of evil in any situation.

With God, you can prevail against the pressure to worship at the table of false gods.

Establishing Christ's Presence in Your World

What is the one thing in your workplace or community you would most like to see changed? Identify who is in charge or has the authority to make this change. Identify who might help you construct a creative alternative to the way things are being done. Identify others who might go with you to those in authority. Identify clearly the time frame, means of making a decision, and benefits to those in authority that are a part of your alternate plan.

Take courage and act!

Reflect or Discuss

- What is likely to happen if certain things that should be changed aren't?
- How important is it for us to present alternate plans politely, offering reasonable tests of how the alternate plans work, and no loss of perceived authority for those who are in power?

Don't cry for change without a plan for the change you desire to see.

CHAPTER FIVE

You Can Know the Truth That Sets You Free

Nothing gives a student more joy than getting word that he has passed a difficult exam or that he has finished a course with a passing grade.

The greater truth is, nothing will ever give a person more joy than hearing the Lord give a passing grade in eternity: "Well done, you good and faithful servant." Nothing is more valuable or more worthy of our pursuit!

We can learn some important lessons from Daniel and his friends.

First, the good news. They passed the test!

The Bible tells us that after ten days of eating only vegetables and drinking only water, Daniel and his friends looked "healthier and better nourished than any

[Jesus said,] If you hold to my teaching, you are really my disciples. Then you will know the truth, and the truth will set you free.

(JOHN 8:31–32)

of the young men who ate the royal food" (Dan. 1:15). This was the test that Daniel had set up for himself and his patrons with the men who were supervising their training in Babylon. Because they passed, they were allowed to eat vegetables and water for the rest of their training program.

The reward was not just an extra helping of vegetables, however. God also gave them a passing grade and good rewards. The Bible says, "To these four young men God gave knowledge and understanding of all kinds of literature and learning. And Daniel could understand visions and dreams of all kinds" (Dan. 1:17).

This reward meant that these young men not only had good reading comprehension and memory, but they had real understanding about how to apply what they had learned without breaking any of God's commandments. They knew how to discern what God desired, even as they gained knowledge about what their captors required. They had acquired the wisdom of knowing how to function effectively and righteously in an environment that stinks to high heaven.

The Knowledge God Imparts

There's a very important principle here and I don't want you to overlook it. Daniel and his friends were given two very distinct kinds of knowledge and understanding as a result of their obedience. He will do the same for you.

1. KNOWLEDGE OF GOD'S COMMANDMENTS

When you obey God, the Lord rewards you first and foremost with increased understanding about the commandments of God. The more you obey God, the more you want to obey and see a need to obey. Your understanding about the commandments of God and the importance of keeping them *grows* the more you obey.

When I was a young boy, I was allowed to do certain things and not to do many other things. Like all young boys I thought, *When I grow up, I'm going to do these things my parents are telling me I can't do, and nobody is going to tell me I can't.* The truth is, the older I became, I discovered even more things I could not do, not because my parents told me I couldn't do them, but because God's Word told me I should not do them! When you obey God and receive the rewards related to that obedience, you will have a desire to obey God even more. As a friend of mine says, "You want to obey the *details* of God's Word."

2. KNOWLEDGE OF THE WORLD

The Lord also rewards a person who obeys Him with knowledge and understanding about the world. These four Hebrew guys were given knowledge about "all kinds of literature and learning" (Dan. 1:17). They were able to learn the materials their captors were presenting to them, but with an added ability: they could perceive right from wrong in that literature, and they knew how to apply what was good and discard what was wrong. If we have ever needed that ability, we need it today! So many theories and falsehoods are presented to us, not only in our schools but in the media on a daily basis, that we need to be able to discern very clearly, "That's true," "That's only speculation," and "That's an outright lie."

Do You Know What to Obey?

The real question facing us is this: do we know what God has commanded so we might obey His commandments?

Daniel and his friends knew the Torah—the books of the Law given to Moses—and the writings of the prophets. Make no mistake about that. They really knew God's Word. They had studied it diligently as boys. Given the age they were when they were carted off to Babylon, they may have already passed their bar mitzvah exams or they may have been on the verge of taking them. They may even have been in Jerusalem for the purpose of taking these exams, which the temple priests usually conducted. Believe me, these exams were just as strenuous—if not more so—than anything Nebuchadnezzar could come up with.

To prepare for Torah exams, boys the age of these young men were expected to have memorized the Torah, ideally the entire book and minimally vast portions of it. The Torah includes the books of the Bible we know as Genesis, Exodus, Leviticus, Numbers, and Deuteronomy. That's an amazing feat!

Not only did these four Hebrew young men know the Law and writings of the prophets very well, but they also were very familiar with the Psalms and likely sang them at every opportunity.

In addition, they had been trained to live out the Law in their everyday lives—in the way they ate, the feasts they kept, the rituals in which they participated. They didn't just have head knowledge about the commands of God, they had *life knowledge* about how to obey the commands and worship God in their daily lives. They knew about moral absolutes because they lived by moral absolutes.

So, Daniel and his friends were prepared. They knew how to study and how to learn. They knew how to apply what they learned. They were given added ability.

"But what," you may be asking, "about all those vegetables?"

A Diet of Vegetables in Babylon

Was there any advantage to a diet of vegetables for Daniel and his friends there in the king's palace in Babylon? Absolutely! God always deals in the practical matters of life as well as the spiritual.

FOOD FOR CLEAR THINKING

The rich food and wine of the king's palace were very likely loaded with sugar and fat. Babylonians gave such foods to the pagan gods because they were foods human beings considered to be delicacies, and therefore, the gods must surely have thought they were delicacies, too! From a very practical nutritional standpoint, this kind of food puts a person to sleep! Think about it. After a big Thanksgiving dinner loaded with rich foods, what's the first thing a person feels like doing? Taking a nap! Days and days of rich feasting make thinking slower, reasoning more muddied, and memory foggier. Science is proving this more and more. Daniel and his friends had an added ability to learn with clear minds.

FOOD FOR A CLEAR CONSCIENCE

Second, eating these foods gave Daniel and his friends a clear conscience before God. They knew they were in right standing with God because they were obeying Him and putting Him first. Therefore, they could learn what was put before them without any emotional or psychological baggage.

People who are bound up emotionally or psychologically often have real learning problems, and especially so when it comes to applying what they have learned in ways that are not only wise but productive and efficient. They often don't know how to prioritize or determine what they should store in long-term memory. Emotions can cloud reasoning ability. Behavioral scientists are proving these conclusions more and more. Daniel and his friends were freed up to use their brains fully.

INCREASED INFLUENCE

Third, because Daniel had won his point about being allowed to eat vegetables and drink water, he no doubt discovered that he could request other things from his captors, as long as he held to reason and did not rebel against his captors' authority. This is true for any person who begins to establish a track record in a job or organization. If one idea that a person suggests works, then a second idea from that person is more quickly entertained and acted upon.

I have no doubt that as the years passed, Daniel established a growing reputation with his captors as a young man who could be counted on to come up with solutions, innovations, and leading-edge technology. How do I know this? Because that is what happens all around us in various organizations today! Those who think quickly and with clarity, without emotional baggage or spiritual sin to weigh them down, advance in the companies in which they find themselves. They are the ones hired more quickly and promoted more readily. They are the ones ready with a solution, idea, or answer when someone at the top has a request or need.

Now, you may be thinking that I am setting you up to become a vegetarian. Not at all. This eating plan was important for Daniel and his friends in the king's palace in Babylon. What I do know is that God has a plan for the way in which you are to walk out your obedience to His commands in the place where you live, work, and worship. Your obedience will likely result in your giving up some things that others around you seem to be enjoying. To obey God fully, you may not be able to do everything your colleagues or peers are doing, and you may not be able to go every place they go. In exchange for your obedience, God will reward you greatly in your ability to learn and understand, and He will do this in very practical ways.

Facing the King's Exam

In addition to passing the initial test regarding their eating plan—which was like a first exam for them—Daniel and his friends did extremely well when it came to their final exam before the king. The Bible tells us that at the end of the three-year course Nebuchadnezzar had established, the chief official presented these four young Hebrew men to the king himself. The Bible says, "The king talked with them, and he found none equal to Daniel, Hananiah, Mishael, and Azariah; so they entered the king's service" (Dan. 1:19).

This audience with Nebuchadnezzar doesn't seem to have fazed Daniel and his friends in any way. They were apparently very fluent in their ability to discuss many issues with the king. And talk about pass a test! The Bible goes on to say, "In every matter of wisdom and understanding about which the king questioned them, he found them ten times better than all the magicians and enchanters in his whole kingdom" (Dan. 1:20). Daniel and his friends not only were better than their fellow students in their understanding and wisdom. They were better than all of the old pros among the Chaldeans! Ten times better!

What can we conclude from these few verses?

First, Daniel and his friends were free to think in that hour. They had a lightning-speed ability to reason and come quickly to answers and solutions. They knew their facts. They had years of preparation in this—they had studied and learned their courses very well with a clear mind. They were free to think fast on their feet.

Second, Daniel and his friends had nothing to hide emotionally or spiritually. Therefore, they were very quick to discuss virtually any issue the king mentioned. They felt free to speak up. Nebuchadnezzar might have been the big boss in that room, but in the heart of Daniel, the Big Boss was the One whom they he trusted and served every day, not just this one particular day.

Freedom to think clearly; freedom to speak up: what powerful freedoms these are! The person who has these freedoms is truly *free*! He doesn't hesitate when it comes to knowing what is true, right, and good. He's not reluctant to speak up for what is true, right, and good. He doesn't fish around for approval from other people—he acts immediately on what is true, right, and good.

When you come to the place where you are "free indeed"—free of doubt and confusion so you can think clearly, and free of emotional or psychological baggage so you can be free to speak up— God will put you in positions where you will have authority to establish behaviors based upon God's commandments. Look for it to happen!

You don't have to create opportunities to exert the power of one. God allows you to have those opportunities! They come as part of the ebb and flow of everyday life. Your challenge and mine is to recognize that we have been given an opportunity and we have freedom in Christ Jesus—and then to boldly seize the opportunity!

Establishing Christ's Presence in Your World

The beginning point for true freedom in speaking and acting lies in obeying God. In what area of your life are you not obeying God as completely as you can or should? What changes do you need to make in your life to obey God fully? Take action today to *obey*.

Is there something God wants you to learn? Start learning it.

Is there something God wants you to say to someone? Make an appointment to say what it is God wants you to say.

Is there something God wants you to start or renew in your life? Take a first step toward doing that—now, within the next twenty-four hours.

Reflect or Discuss

- Reflect back over your life. When has your obedience to God put you a little at odds with people around you? What has been the reward of your obedience?

God wants you to be *free* to think without confusion or doubt, and to speak up whenever necessary.

CHAPTER SIX

You Can Live a Life Free of Fear

Have you ever found yourself suddenly in a spotlight, gripped by fear? I'm not talking about being in a theatrical play and forgetting your lines, although that would certainly strike fear into the heart of just about every person I know. I'm talking about being given a platform to speak and the focus is on you. Have you ever experienced a time when all eyes in the room suddenly turned to you to see what you would say or do?

Fear is common to all people, and some fears are natural. You should be afraid of walking out into traffic, stepping too close to the edge of a cliff, or touching a red-hot stove. Other fears, however, are not ones God desires His people to have. These are the paralyzing

Hear me, O God . . .
protect my life from the
threat of the enemy.
. . . Let the righteous rejoice
in the LORD
and take refuge in him.
(PSALM 64:1, 10)

fears that come from confusion and a lack of faith. The apostle Paul wrote to Timothy very clearly on this: "God did not give us a spirit of timidity, but a spirit of power, of love, and of self-discipline" (2 Tim. 1:7). God expects us to have the courage to speak up because we are putting our trust in God, not in our audience. We are trusting God to fill us with His power and His love and to show us clearly His plan so we can walk in it.

God gave Daniel and his three friends, Hananiah, Mishael, and Azariah, a special ability to learn and understand as a result of their obedience. God set them free from confusion about right and wrong. He set them free from the emotional baggage associated with wondering if they were obeying God or not obeying Him. Their obedience resulted in an ability to think and speak freely and clearly.

There was yet another benefit to their obedience, and that was this: their obedience put them in a position to know God better. Did you notice I did not say "know *about* God"? I said "know God."

Knowing about God and knowing God are two very different things.

Knowing God is not something you can learn from books. It is something you can experience only by reading what He said about Himself and then applying it to your life, day in and day out, month in and month out, year in and year out. It is something that comes by "walking the walk" with the Lord, and not just talking the talk. It comes by prayer and spending intimate quiet times with the Lord, listening to what He might speak deep within your heart and soul.

It is in this way that a person truly comes to know the fullness of what God has promised, what God expects, and what God has planned for his or her life, as well as what God has planned for the ages.

I grew up in a Christian home, and I am eternally thankful for that. I grew up knowing the Bible stories. I heard sermons that clearly presented the principles of God. I grew up seeing my parents' examples of faithfulness to God. As a child and young man, I knew a lot about God. But it was only after I personally came to know Jesus Christ as my personal Savior—accepting that what He did on the cross was for the forgiveness of my sins—that I began to know God. It was at that point that my relationship with the Lord took on greater meaning.

Before a person accepts Jesus as Savior, God seems remote and, very often, is perceived to be a mean judge just waiting to pronounce severe punishment for sin. After a person accepts Jesus as Savior, God becomes close, accessible, and a loving Father who desires the highest and best for His children.

Before a person accepts Jesus as Savior, God's ways and purposes seem unknowable. After a person accepts Jesus as Savior, the light begins to come on as a person reads the Bible. The believer begins to experience what the Bible calls a "renewal" of the mind.

Before a person accepts Jesus as Savior, it often seems very difficult to show love to God—a person is always wondering how good he can try to be, and how much good he must do. After accepting Jesus as Savior, a person is free to praise and thank God, knowing that salvation is a free gift from a loving God, not a matter of good works.

Obeying God by accepting Jesus as Savior is the first key to knowing God.

But what about things in Daniel's time?

In that time, six hundred years before Jesus was born, the only way a young Hebrew man could know God was to obey God, to be faithful in praying to God, and to develop a track record of trusting in God. That's what Daniel and his friends did and continued to do.

The book of Daniel doesn't tell us that Daniel and his friends met daily for prayer and study of the Torah, but we do know that at the first sign of difficulty, these four friends resorted to prayer. A person doesn't turn first to prayer if that isn't a pattern already established in his or her life. We do know that when Daniel and his friends prayed, they knew the attributes and nature of the One to whom they were praying. That kind of prayer doesn't come from the lips of a person who doesn't know God.

We also know this: the Lord gave Daniel an additional ability to "understand visions and dreams of all kinds" (Dan. 1:17). This was spiritual knowledge about the ways in which God works, and the reasons for His actions. Daniel was able to differentiate between godly and ungodly schemes. He could see into God's purposes and God's desires. Ultimately that is the type of knowledge every believer in Christ Jesus desires. We want to know that we are on target with what God desires for us and those around us. We want to know that we are on track with what God is doing in us, through us, and all around us.

The truth of God's Word from cover to cover is that God reveals Himself to people according to the consistency and steadfastness of their obedience. He entrusts those who obey Him with an enlarged understanding of His nature.

Through the first few years of their captivity in Babylon, Daniel and his small band of followers appear to have matured in their faith to the place where they trusted God with every aspect of their lives. They appear to have had no anxiety in their hearts about an audience with the king. They seem free of all fear.

Freedom from fear is what happens when a person has *faith*.

Faith Overcomes Fear

Why does the devil spend so much time trying to instill fear in people? Because he knows that those who are filled with fear don't have faith. Faith is required if a person is going to have the courage to speak up for the truth and to obey God in spite of cultural-crunch pressure.

From my many years of studying the Bible and being a pastor, let me give you a little insight into how I perceive the devil works.

Before the devil tempts people, he seeks to undermine their confidence in God and to confuse them. People who lack confidence in what they know or whom they know are people who are fearful. People who don't know the truth of God's commandments or the truth of God's nature are people who get easily led astray and have trouble thinking clearly. Such people are always second-guessing: *Is this the right thing to do? Who will approve of me or like me if I say this? Who will criticize me or reject me if I do that?* When the devil has people feeling scared and confused, it's at that point he throws his strongest temptation at them.

There's nothing new in this strategy. The devil has been doing this since the Garden of Eden. It's a tactic he's used through the ages. Why? Because it works! At least it works on most people. The devil goes after those who don't know God's Word and don't know God in a personal relationship. The devil uses lies to instill confusion and doubt. He causes a person to question the love and the absolutes of God. He tries to generate concern for peer approval and a reluctance to speak up or stand up and be noticed.

Fear keeps a person from making decisions, voicing opinions, or offering suggestions. Fear keeps a person from taking a stand.

The Cure for Fear and Confusion

The cure for confusion and fear is threefold:

1. KNOW GOD'S WORD
Read and study God's Word. That's the only way to know what God says!

2. BE STRONG IN YOUR RELATIONSHIP WITH THE LORD
Spend time with Him daily in prayer and quiet reflection on His Word.

3. DEVELOP A TRACK RECORD OF TRUSTING
Do what God says to do. Obey Him. Apply the Word of God to your life. Live it out. See how God works when you put your faith in Him to direct you, deal with those who persecute you, and show His love to you. God wants you and every person who believes in Jesus Christ to be strong in faith and to live free of fear! He wants you to trust Him with every part of your being—spirit, mind, and emotions. When faith is strong, fear evaporates.

The person who trusts God rests assured that God is responsible for the outcome and consequences of anything that person may experience. God is in total control. The person doesn't need to micromanage his plans for the future. He simply needs to trust the Lord and do what He puts in his path to do.

Daniel and his friends displayed no fear in meeting with Nebuchadnezzar. Most people in Babylon would have been very nervous about a face-to-face encounter—much less an oral examination—with this man, the greatest emperor of that day. This would be like having an appointment with the president of the United States, the chief justice of the Supreme Court, the leaders of the Senate and House of Representatives, the most prominent journalists of the most powerful media outlets, and Donald Trump and Alan Greenspan all in one sitting!

These four Hebrew teenagers took it all in stride. They didn't panic. They no doubt showed respect to the king, but they did not worship him. They worshiped God alone and they did what they did to please God, not Nebuchadnezzar.

Rather than be awed by Nebuchadnezzar, these young men impressed the emperor. He gave them positions in the king's service. He could call upon them whenever he desired. They had responsibility and authority, very likely positions that many of the Babylonians thought were beyond their years. Daniel and his friends had the trust of Nebuchadnezzar, but even more importantly, they were in a trust relationship with God. They had learned to steadily trust God.

God, in turn, trusted Daniel, Hananiah, Mishael, and Azariah to remain consistent in leadership posts, just as they had remained consistent during their training period. Nebuchadnezzar may have appointed them to specific posts, but it was God who had raised them up, and they knew it.

The apostle Paul knew this power of God in his life as well. He wrote to the Corinthians:

> We do not want you to be uninformed, brothers, about the hardships we suffered in the province of Asia. We were under great pressure, far beyond our ability to endure, so that we despaired even of life. Indeed, in our hearts we felt

the sentence of death. But this happened that we might not rely on ourselves but on God, who raises the dead. He has delivered us from such a deadly peril, and he will deliver us. On him we have set our hope that he will continue to deliver us. (2 Corinthians 1:8–10)

Are you scared of something or someone today? Is fear holding you back from speaking up or taking a stand? Check your faith level. Check the degree to which you know God's Word, are in relationship with God, and have developed a track record of trusting God in all things. Begin to trust Him to deliver you from all fear, and from anything that seems to be a threat to you!

Establishing Christ's Presence in Your World

Is there something God wants you to establish as a new habit or spiritual discipline so you might come to know God better? Get up a half hour earlier tomorrow morning and start doing it. (You may need to go to bed a half hour earlier tonight so you can do this!)

Reflect or Discuss

- What strikes fear into your heart today? In what ways might this fear challenge you to trust God more and thus cause your faith to grow? Is it possible that God is using this fear to teach you a faith lesson?
- Reflect back over your life. How has your confidence in the Lord grown the more you have walked in His ways by obeying His commandments and being faithful in the tasks to which God has called you? In what ways has your faith in God's love and trustworthiness grown?

The Lord desires for you to walk in faith, not fear, in all situations and before all people.

CHAPTER SEVEN

You Can Make Loyal Friendships

Every person I know wants to have a good friend. A desire for friendship seems to be built into us as human beings. One of the greatest compliments that a husband or wife can give is to say, "My spouse is my best friend." Let me assure you, that is the way I feel about my wife.

Don't you know that friendship with the world is hatred toward God?

(JAMES 4:4)

This need for friendship in our lives is at the root of what Jesus said to His disciples on the night before His crucifixion: "I no longer call you servants, because a servant does not know his master's business. Instead, I have called you friends, for everything that I learned from my Father I have made known to you." Jesus also said, "Greater love has no one than this, that he lay down his life for his friends" (John 15:15, 13). Jesus is our

Friend of friends, just as He is King of kings and Lord of lords. He is our supreme Friend.

The Hallmarks of Friendship

What does it mean to have a friend? There are four hallmarks of a genuine friendship:

1. AVAILABILITY

Friends are there for each other. A friend is a person who will stick with you when you face difficult times. A friend will also be there to applaud your accomplishments. A friend is someone you can reach in a crisis.

Christ Jesus is always available to us—He always has time for us. He does not leave us or reject us. The promise of God in both the Old and New Testaments is this: "Never will I leave you; never will I forsake you" (Heb. 13:5; see Deut. 31:6). Therefore, we can say with the writer of Hebrews, "The Lord is my helper; I will not be afraid. / What can man do to me?" (Heb. 13:6).

2. COMMUNICATION

Friends talk to each other. They share their innermost feelings, dreams, and hopes. They do not withhold information that could be helpful to each other. They are vulnerable in sharing their weaknesses, failures, and fears. They tell what they know about the nature and goodness of God because they know that the better their friends know God and trust God, the more blessings their friends will receive in their lives here and in eternity.

For a Christian, a true friend is a person with whom you can communicate your faith. A woman talked to me not long ago about a person she thought might become a friend. She said, "I discovered through the months of our getting better acquainted that this woman clammed up every time I brought up the name of Jesus. I felt sadness in my heart each time this happened. The Lord eventually showed me that this woman was not a real Christian, even though she went to church occasionally. She had no real desire to know Jesus. I found it very difficult to continue in our relationship, except to try to win her to Christ. I knew she couldn't really be my friend if we couldn't share faith in the Lord."

3. ENCOURAGEMENT

Friends build each other up. They don't reject each other or carry resentments and anger. Rather, they speak positive words to each other. They freely forgive and are generous in their words of praise and appreciation.

A true friend will tell you when you are making a mistake or are falling short of your potential, not to put you down but so you might make better choices and become everything God has created you to be!

4. LOYALTY

Friends are loyal to each other. They don't rat on each other or participate in gossip or schemes that might hurt each other.

Friendships take time to build. You may be attracted to a person quickly, and you may like a person for some time, but to have a genuine friendship, you need to go through some of life's experiences together. You need to have some history in your friendship to know if a person truly will be available to you, communicate with you, encourage you, and be loyal to you.

Beware of False Friends

A false friend is a person who may appear to be a friend, but in truth, he is only an admirer or an acquaintance. At times a false friend may be someone who is seeking to manipulate you or mislead you willfully or subconsciously.

When we read the opening verses of the book of Daniel, it may appear that Daniel had become friends with one or more of his captors. God's Word says that the official in charge of Daniel's well-being in the king's palace showed "favor and sympathy to Daniel."

That sounds like friendship, but it wasn't. This verse in Daniel also tells us, "God had caused the official to show favor and sympathy to Daniel" (Dan. 1:9).

Just because somebody appears to admire you, wants to be with you, seems to empathize with your situation or problem, shows sympathy to you, or helps you in some way does not mean that this person is a friend. It may mean that God has used that person to help you, not that God has sent that person to you for a long-term relationship. Not every person who is friendly is destined to be a person with whom you can or should share your innermost feelings and ideas, to whom you should be loyal, or with whom you should spend time or enter into a partnership of some kind.

You certainly can be friendly to acquaintances and admirers, and you can respond to their interest in you by sharing the gospel with them, but you must not become allied with them, especially if they are not believers in Christ (2 Cor. 6:14; James 4:4).

If more people understood the importance of building genuine friendships based upon God's principles — and if they understood that not every friendly person can or should be a friend — there would be considerably less anger and bitterness in the world, and probably far fewer lawsuits and divorces!

Four Friends in a Time of Trouble

Daniel, Hananiah, Mishael, and Azariah were friends. There is little doubt that Daniel was the leader of this group. Most Bible scholars believe that Daniel was the eldest of the four. Daniel spoke on their behalf.

One of the most important statements I can make to you about the power of one is this: your first job is to influence just one other person to stand with you in believing what is right. Make a godly friend!

That person will be your godly ally. That person will pray for you, encourage you, and stand by your side.

In all likelihood, if you influence one other person to stand with you, you soon will have a small group standing with you. The group may not ever be large—it doesn't necessarily need to be.

The person you influence first may be a relative, even a sibling. It may be a spouse. It may be a friend.

Influence one—then the two of you influence others.

Moses had Aaron at his side when he went to confront Pharaoh.

David had Jonathan as his friend and ally.

Paul had Barnabas, and later Silas, and later Timothy and Titus.

Jesus started with just two men interested in knowing more about Him. One of them was Andrew, who influenced his brother, Peter.

The pattern appears throughout the Bible. Don't seek to change the world overnight or to influence masses at the outset. Seek to find and influence *one person*. That's your starting point! Ecclesiastes 4:9–12 tells us:

Two are better than one,
Because they have a good reward for their labor.
For if they fall, one will lift up his companion.
. . . If two lie down together, they will keep warm. . . .
Though one may be overpowered by another, two can
   withstand him.
And a threefold cord is not quickly broken.
(NKJV)

We see this clearly in Daniel's life! Note what happened next!

A severe problem arose in the palace. Nebuchadnezzar had a dream that greatly troubled him. He called all of the magicians, enchanters, sorcerers, and astrologers in the region to tell him what he had dreamed.

Did you notice that Nebuchadnezzar was not asking these advisers to give him the meaning of a dream? Nebuchadnezzar couldn't remember what he had dreamed! He only knew that he had awakened extremely troubled and that he could not go back to sleep. He wanted his spiritual gurus to tell him what he had dreamed and then tell him what the dream meant. They couldn't do this, of course, and they told him so. Nebuchadnezzar wasn't amused. He immediately accused them of conspiracy and threatened them with death if they didn't do as he had requested.

The astrologers said, "There isn't a guy on earth who can do what you ask! Only the gods can do this and they don't live in the palace" (see Dan. 2:10–11). This response made Nebuchadnezzar so angry that he ordered the immediate execution of all the wise men of Babylon. Daniel, Hananiah, Mishael, and Azariah were among those wise men!

As soon as Daniel saw the executioners leave the palace in search of the wise men who were in the king's service, he asked Arioch, the commander of the king's guard, why the king had issued such a harsh decree. The Bible tells us Daniel spoke with "wisdom and tact" (Dan. 2:14). Arioch responded to this way of speaking — most people will tell you what you want to know if you treat them with respect and ask politely for information — and he told Daniel about the king's dream and his conversation with the astrologers.

Daniel immediately went back to his house and explained the situation to his three disciples. What did Daniel ask them to do? Pray! Daniel "urged them to plead for mercy from the God of heaven concerning this mystery, so that he and his friends might not be executed with the rest of the wise men of Babylon" (Dan. 2:18).

If you have any question about whether a person is a real friend or a false friend, here's the test: ask the person to pray for God's mercy on your behalf. A real friend will have no hesitation in doing so. I know that from personal experience. On countless occasions as I have attempted to discern and obey the Lord's leading in my life and in my ministry, I have called upon trusted friends to pray with me. Their prayers have been invaluable!

I don't have any doubt that these four friends prayed until they got the answer from heaven. They didn't pray for just a few minutes — their lives were on the line! They prayed long into the night. They prayed with intensity because they had to have an answer from the Lord. They were bonded in prayer. It was the highest and best expression of their loyalty to each other, their ability to encourage each other, their communication with each other, and their availability to each other.

Why do you need friends? Again, because friends are part of God's plan for bringing you from places of disaster to places of victory. God's Word tells us that one man with God's help might put a thousand to flight, but two with God's help might put ten thousand to flight (Deut. 32:30).

In exercising the power of one, you need friends who will help you in your walk with Christ—friends who will pray with you and for you, minister alongside you, help you grow in your faith, and worship with you.

The power of having a friend alongside is vital as you take a stand for the truth. A friend by your side can give you just the courage you need to speak up and take action.

If you don't have a godly friend, ask the Lord to bring such a friend into your life and treat that friend as Christ treats you; with respect, loyalty, encouragement, and a willingness to be vulnerable in communicating. Your power of one can be of greater impact when you have a praying friend or two.

If you already have a godly friend, do things that will strengthen and deepen that friendship: spend time together, pray and witness for the Lord together, talk together about subjects that are close to your heart and close to the heart of God, and speak words that are inspirational and uplifting.

The Power of One? Or Power of Two?

"But why," you may be asking, "did you title this book *Discover the Power of One* if it really takes two or more to get the job done effectively?"

In the first place, as a Christian, you aren't just one. You have the power of the Lord on your side so in a very real way, you are already operating in the strength of two—and actually, that's two to the unlimited power of God's strength, wisdom, and love! You are in a friendship with God, and it is this friendship with Him that empowers you to do more than you can ever do by yourself.

God does not just call you to friendship with Himself, however.

He also calls you to be part of a body of believers. He calls you to extend friendship to others even as you receive friendship from them. Soon you will discover that the power of one is far more powerful than you thought possible.

As a Christian, one of your top priorities must be to become the strongest witness you can possibly be for the truth of God's Word and the Gospel of Jesus Christ. To gain strength in your witness, you need to make friends!

So many Christians think they must go it alone. It is very difficult for those who have to exercise the power of one alone — those who are involuntarily isolated. But whenever possible, seek followers. Daniel did. You need friends within the church you attend, so make the effort to get to know people, do things with people, give to people of your time, talents, and resources, and seek to make friends. Be there for your church friends. Receive the help they offer to you.

The power of one begins with you. It doesn't end there.

Establishing Christ's Presence in Your World

Call a friend today and make a plan to get together. Let your friend know that you value your friendship. Speak words of encouragement, appreciation, and admiration for the godly qualities you see in your friend.

Pray with a friend about a problem that you both perceive in your community, workplace, or families. Go to God together with earnest prayer, joining your faith to believe for God's highest and best answer.

Reflect or Discuss

- What keeps a friendship from growing?
- What keeps a friendship from enduring over time?
- What keeps a friendship from being as meaningful as you believe a friendship can be?
- How might each of these obstacles to friendship be overcome?

Godly friends are part of God's plan for you.

CHAPTER EIGHT

You Can Experience
the Power of Praise

God gave Daniel the answer Daniel was seeking during a prayer meeting. Daniel and his friends Hananiah, Mishael, and Azariah were diligently pleading for mercy from God as they faced a death threat from King Nebuchadnezzar. The king had demanded that the wise men of Babylon tell him what he had dreamed and then interpret the dream. Daniel knew that God alone could resolve that problem.

God has already enabled you to solve many problems in this life. He has given you the wisdom of His Word and His commandments. He has equipped you with various life experiences, friends to be your mentors and wise counselors, and leaders in the church to preach the Word

I will praise you with the harp
for your faithfulness, O my
God;
I will sing praise to you
with the lyre,
O Holy One of Israel.
My lips will shout for joy
when I sing praise to you—
I, whom you have redeemed.
(PSALM 71:22–23)

and teach you how to live in a godly manner. For most problems you will face, God has already given the answer if you will open your eyes, diligently search the Word, or remember what you have been taught. A man once said that 75 percent of all sermons are simply reminders of what we have already been told. I suspect that's true.

The problem is that many of us are too lazy to seek out answers. We want them handed to us on a silver platter. Even if the answer comes, we sometimes are reluctant to act on it out of fear that we may make a mistake or that we may be held accountable for our actions. Accept the fact that God has given you His Word and a good mind with which to read it and study it. Act on the answers He reveals to you.

Very few problems disappear on their own. A problem may disappear only to go underground in your emotions or the emotions of other people. When it resurfaces, look out. The problem is likely to erupt explosively and be far worse than before! God intends that we address and solve most problems, and God gives us the ability to do so.

Some problems only God can sort out. He alone knows the beginning from the ending. He alone knows the ways and means that He has prepared to get you through a difficult circumstance, all the way to the conclusion that will bring relief to you and glory to Him.

God's Deliverance

Daniel and his friends were facing just such a problem. They went to prayer about the matter and although the Bible doesn't say so directly, the implication is clearly that they prayed until the answer came. The Bible says, "During the night the mystery was revealed to Daniel in a vision" (Dan. 2:19). This verse doesn't say that the mystery was revealed in a dream, which would imply that Daniel was asleep. It says the mystery was revealed in a vision, very likely while Daniel was awake and praying!

What was Daniel's first response?

He praised God!

Daniel didn't praise God for the answer per se.

He didn't praise God for giving him the words he needed to speak to Nebuchadnezzar.

He praised God for *who God is.*

That's the very essence of praise. We thank God for what He does, gives, and has promised to do and give. We *praise* God for who He is.

Daniel began his praise this way:

> Praise be to the name of God
>   for ever and ever;
>   wisdom and power are his.
> He changes times and seasons;
>   he sets up kings and deposes them.
> He gives wisdom to the wise
>   and knowledge to the discerning.
> He reveals deep and hidden things;
>   he knows what lies in darkness,
>   and light dwells with him.
>
> (DANIEL 2:20–22)

Daniel made no claim to have wisdom and power of his own. He knew that God was the source of wisdom and power.

It's amazing to me how many people today believe they have achieved success, wealth, or an educational level totally on their own ability. Nothing could be farther from the truth!

You can't accomplish anything in life without God's giving you the health, intelligence, opportunities, and resources to pursue a goal and reach it.

The Lord is worthy of our praise for all things and in all things. He is our Creator, Sustainer, Provider, Protector, and our Ever-Present Help. Daniel knew it. We need to know it too.

God's Answer

Only after Daniel had praised the Lord for *who He is* did Daniel thank the Lord for giving him the answer to his prayer. He said:

> I thank and praise you, O God of my fathers;
>   You have given me wisdom and power,
> you have made known to me what we asked of you,
>   you have made known to us the dream of the king.
> (DANIEL 2:23)

Daniel could see clearly that the Lord had given him a portion of what the Lord had: wisdom and power.

WISDOM

Daniel knew the dream. God had sovereignly revealed to him what Nebuchadnezzar had dreamed. Daniel knew the *what* of the situation. He had the answer he needed.

POWER

Daniel knew that God was imparting to him the courage to go to the king with this wisdom. Sometimes we can know *what* to do. We can know the cause or the nature of a problem. We can know the solution. It takes great courage, however, to express what we know. It takes power to get up from our knees and walk to a person who is struggling and say, "I know what to do."

Praise Imparts Power to Take Action

How does praise impart the power of God that results in action?

First, praise connects you to God as nothing else can. It points out to you in your own spirit who God is, and who you aren't. When you get a very clear picture of who God is in relationship to you—and that He has all the wisdom and power you need, that He delights in giving you some of His wisdom and power to use, and that He desires the very best for your life as you act on what He gives you—you can't help but be filled with awe.

No matter the nature of the problem—God has an answer!

No matter how difficult the situation—God can make a way where there is no way!

No matter how dire the circumstances—God can change them!

God's Word tells us that Jesus' name is above the names we might give to all sorts of problems. Jesus has a name that is

> far above all rule and authority, power and dominion, and every title that can be given, not only in the present age but also in the one to come. And God placed all things under his feet and appointed him to be head over everything for the church, which is his body, the fullness of him who fills everything in every way. (Ephesians 1:21–23)

God has exalted Jesus

> to the highest place
>   and gave him the name that is above every name,
> that at the name of Jesus every knee should bow,
>   in heaven and on earth and under the earth,
> and every tongue confess that Jesus Christ is Lord,
>   to the glory of God the Father.
>
> (PHILIPPIANS 2:9–11)

Jesus' name is *higher* than sickness . . . rejection . . . alienation . . . strife . . . hatred . . . prejudice . . . pain . . . sorrow . . . hunger . . . abuse . . . poverty. For any problem or negative condition you can think of, He has a name that is higher than that problem or condition. It is the name of Jesus.

When you praise the name of Jesus, you are getting things in right order! You are declaring to your own soul and spirit that you know without a shadow of a doubt who is *really* in control of this world and all the problems in it. You are declaring to your own mind that you know on whom you must rely for all the answers and solutions you need.

And then, when you get that picture clearly in your mind and heart, the awe that you feel gives you a surge of confidence like nothing else can. God is on *your* side! God wants *your* best! God seeks to help *you* in all the areas where you cannot help yourself! God wants to see *you* succeed even if all the odds are against you!

A Surge of Strength and Joy

This great confidence in knowing you are connected to God results in pure joy, regardless of the circumstances you face. Praise is the key to living in joy and responding with joy to everything in life. The Bible tells us that the *joy* of the Lord is directly related to our strength. Read these words from the Psalms:

The LORD is my strength and my song;
    he has become my salvation.
(PSALM 118:14)

I love you, O LORD, my strength.
    . . . I call to the LORD, who is worthy of praise,
and I am saved from my enemies.
(PSALM 18:1, 3)

Sing for joy to God our strength.
(PSALM 81:1)

Throughout the Psalms, we find that those who have joy in the Lord experience God's saving, delivering, and protective strength.

My grandfather, Oza, was a building contractor and a lay leader in the Brethren church to which my mother's family belonged. He lived in a small apartment adjacent to the home of my uncle. When I spent the night with my cousins, I'd sometimes awaken during the night to hear my grandfather praising the Lord in a loud voice.

I couldn't help but wonder why my grandfather was so full of joy. He had lost two sons when they were in their early thirties. He lost his wife while he was a relatively young man. Even so, until he died at the age of ninety-two, he never ceased to praise God throughout the night and then again in the morning. It was praise, not life's circumstances, that gave my grandfather a heart filled with joy and the courage to continue to live and work and stay devoted to God in everything he did.

The link between joy and confident strength is very clear:

- The more you praise God, the more you feel confident in your heart that you are connected to the King of the universe—the God who hung the stars in space and holds all power in His hand.
- The more you praise God, the more you feel excitement about doing what God calls you to do because you know that with God as your ever-present help, you cannot fail!
- The more you praise God, the more empowered you feel to take action that extends God's love, justice, and truth into this world.

Praise empowers us to go to the kings of this earth with a message of repentance, salvation, and discipleship. Praise was the attitude Daniel had as he was ushered into Nebuchadnezzar's presence—it was the very atmosphere in which he moved toward the throne. It is the attitude and atmosphere we must establish for our lives too.

Praise is what will *propel* you to act—it is both the foundation and trigger point for releasing the power of one.

Establishing Christ's Presence in Your World

Spend some time today praising the Lord. Shout His praises. Declare His glory.

Spend even more time tomorrow praising the Lord.

And then spend even more time the next day praising the Lord.

Establish a habit of praise before the Lord. Praise Him all day long. Praise Him in all circumstances. Praise Him when you awaken in the night.

Reflect or Discuss

- After you have spent several weeks with a daily habit of praise, reflect on what this new or enlarged habit of praise is doing inside you. How is praise changing you? In what ways do you feel more humble in God's presence—and yet stronger as you live in this world?
- What are the greatest hindrances you experience as you praise the Lord? What must you do to overcome these hindrances—and why?

Praise empowers God's people.

CHAPTER NINE

You Can Put Yourself Out of a Bully's Target

I was horrified recently to see videotape on a morning newscast of several children beating up another child as they rode a school bus. I have been equally horrified to see prime-time television programs that show children totally out of control: hitting their siblings and their parents in raw rage, seeking to get their own way, no matter the cost.

The word that comes to mind again and again is *bully.* Bullies are people who aggressively mistreat or seek to intimidate other people, generally people they perceive to be weaker and often people who are totally innocent.

Bullying is a huge problem in our world today. It isn't just a matter of children trying to exert power over other

[David said,] Who is this uncircumcised Philistine that he should defy the armies of the living God?

(1 SAMUEL 17:26)

children at school. It is a problem in communities and in the work-place. It is at the core of gangs in our cities. It is at the core of cliques that exclude people who aren't cool enough to be part of the "in" crowd. It is at the core of all segregation and rejection that are based on totally random and external causes that have nothing to do with a person's character or behavior.

Countless children, teens, and adults wake up every morning dreading the day ahead of them because of bullies in their lives.

What makes a person a bully and not just a person who is having a bad day and acting out?

- A bully is a person who has deep anger or frustration.
- A bully is a person who seeks to control and abuse others because he is or has been under the abusive control of someone else.
- A bully is a person who seeks to gain power by making other people feel powerless.
- A bully is a person who repeatedly attempts to manipulate, mistreat, or intimidate other people.
- A bully is a person who seeks to inflict real pain on other people and who is gratified by seeing others suffer physically or emotionally.

The behaviors of a bully are never justified, and they are not rooted in rational, logical reasoning. A bully is acting out of pure emotion, with no regard for consequences associated with his behavior.

Bullying is a pattern of behavior, not just one isolated event. It always begins, however, with one act of bullying, and it is there that we need to confront bullies. People become bullies because they are allowed to become bullies.

Nebuchadnezzar acted as a bully in his treatment of the wise men of Babylon who were unable to tell him what he had dreamed and then interpret the dream. He acted in an irrational way.

When the Chaldeans said to Nebuchadnezzar, "Tell us your dream," the king accused them of stalling for time.

When the Chaldeans told Nebuchadnezzar that his request was unreasonable, the king ordered their execution.

If Daniel and his friends had not prayed and sought God's answer, we probably wouldn't have the book of Daniel. Daniel, Hananiah, Mishael, and Azariah would have been killed along with all the other wise men! King Nebuchadnezzar was a man who was angry, frustrated, and out of control. He acted solely out of emotion. In truth, God had given him a troubling dream—a nightmare—and Nebuchadnezzar responded by trying to make everybody else's life a nightmare!

How to Respond to Bullies

The story of Daniel and his friends gives us three great insights into how we are to respond to bullies.

1. CALL A TIME-OUT

If at all possible, put some space and time between you and the bully. If the bully is at work, take a vacation or a leave of absence. If the bully is at school, ask to be moved to another classroom or another school. If the bully is in the neighborhood, avoid contact as much as possible. Daniel went to Arioch, the commander of the king's guard, to get some insight into Nebuchadnezzar's execution order, and when Daniel knew what the order was all about, he "went in to the king and asked for time, so that he might interpret the dream for him" (Dan. 2:16).

You may not be able to go to a bully directly, but you can seek a time-out from the constant pressure you feel. You may need to go to a person who has authority over the bully, or to an ally who will work with you to get you the time and space you need. Don't delay in this.

In some cases, God may direct you to separate yourself permanently from a bully or a bullying situation. There's no shame in walking away. Jesus told His disciples that if they entered a village and the people there refused to receive them and the gospel they were preaching, they should shake the dust from their feet and walk on. They were not to become emotionally crippled by people who were staunchly opposed to the Good News they were eager to share.

If someone cannot receive you—and Christ who indwells you by the power of His Holy Spirit—then you are free to move on to speak the gospel and live as a Christian in the midst of those who can appreciate the Lord you serve and the person He is molding you to be.

2. BEGIN TO PRAY

Pray for God to deal directly with the bully. Pray for God to give you answers in how you are to relate to the bully. Pray for God's wisdom about what you perhaps should say to other people, especially to those who have power or influence to confront, help, disarm, or persuade the bully. Pray for God to send someone to help you mediate the situation or to be your strong ally.

Jesus gave His disciples a very clear directive about how they were to treat those who persecuted them. He said, "Love your enemies and pray for those who persecute you, that you may be sons of your Father in heaven" (Matt. 5:44). Love your enemies? The apostle Paul put some practical feet to this command of Jesus to love. Love is always active in the Bible. It always involves giving. Paul said, "Bless those who persecute you; bless and do not curse" (Rom. 12:14). In other words, speak positive words to those who seek to do you harm. Do good things for them. Keep a positive attitude. Don't curse them in your heart or with your lips.

3. TAKE A POSITIVE STEP

Do something positive for the person who is seeking to persecute you. This does not mean you need to pay bribes, voice words of false flattery, or try to butter up your enemy. It does mean that you need to take a positive step.

Daniel said to King Nebuchadnezzar: "As you were lying there, O king, your mind turned to things to come, and the revealer of mysteries showed you what is going to happen" (Dan. 2:29). Nebuchadnezzar regarded his dream as terrifying. It gave him high anxiety to the point he couldn't sleep. He was greatly troubled by his dream. Daniel said, in essence, "This dream is a good thing! God has given you this dream so you might see what is about to happen and take action."

Then Daniel spelled out the dream. He told the king that he had dreamed about a large statue that was "dazzling" and "awesome in appearance" (Dan. 2:31). The statue was made of gold, silver, bronze, iron, and clay. A rock smashed the statue's feet. The statue crumbled into pieces and the wind swept it away. Daniel told the king that this dream was about what would happen in the future.

As you pray about a bully in your life, the Lord may very well reveal to you why the person is acting the way he or she does. He may reveal to you deep hurt and insecurity in the person, the real need the person has for love and friendship, or the ultimate consequences the person will face if he continues bullying. Are you to go to the bully with this information? Perhaps. Ask God to show you if that is what He wants you to do—very possibly in the presence of a third person you both have agreed upon to be a mediator or counselor between you.

What you can do in response to what the Lord reveals to you is begin to *act* in a way that will bring healing to the person. God's Word tells us that we must never repay evil for evil. We must continue to do the right things, refusing to act in vengeance. If our enemy is hungry, we are to feed him. If he is thirsty, we are to give him something to drink. We must refuse to be "overcome by evil, but overcome evil with good" (Rom. 12:21).

Try to get to the core of the deep need in the bully's life and what you might do to effectively address that need.

A woman told me not long ago about a bully she was facing at work. Her supervisor was a cruel woman who took every opportunity to dish out criticism and ridicule. This woman took a weekend retreat at a lakeside cabin solely to pray and seek God about what to do. The Lord revealed to her as she prayed that her supervisor was facing an onslaught of abusive criticism and ridicule from her husband — that this treatment had been going on for years and that her supervisor was starved for a positive word.

The woman went to work on Monday morning with a game plan. She determined that every time her supervisor spoke to her in a critical tone of voice or said words of ridicule, she would look her in the eye and give her a positive reply — a word of appreciation for her appearance, her skills, and so forth. She would speak only genuine compliments, seeking out something good she could say, however minor it might be, rather than walk away in silence or cringe in subservience.

This woman said, "The first time I did this, my boss just stared at me and made another critical remark as she turned and stomped away from me. The next time was the same. But the third time she said something critical to me and I replied with a kind compliment, she burst into tears. I was floored. I had an opportunity to tell her that I was sorry for whatever was happening in her life that hurt her so much. And from that day on, she has never made another mean-spirited remark to me. Now I'm looking for some opportunities to see if there might be some way I can help her and minister the love of God to her."

I can't guarantee you those same results, but I can guarantee you this: if you will put some space into your relationship with a bully, ask God to show you what to do and how to do it, and then take the positive step He leads you to take, you will have *God* fully on your side as you deal with the bully. He will act in ways that are totally within His authority and power to act. His ways may be a mystery to you, but trust Him to work on your behalf.

The outcome for Daniel was dramatic. King Nebuchadnezzar "fell prostrate before Daniel and paid him honor and ordered that an offering and incense be presented to him." The king went on to say to Daniel, "Surely your God is the God of gods and the Lord of kings and a revealer of mysteries, for you were able to reveal this mystery" (Dan. 2:46–47).

And then Nebuchadnezzar promoted Daniel to an even higher position and showered him with gifts. Daniel became the ruler over the Babylonian Empire and was put in authority over all the wise men. "At Daniel's request," Nebuchadnezzar made Hananiah, Mishael, and Azariah, the three who were Daniel's compatriots, administrators over Babylon, the capital city. In other words, Daniel exercised the power of one yet again by promoting from within, as it were.

Just the day before, these four young Hebrews were facing an immediate death sentence without any trial or appeal.

Can God turn around a bully situation for you? Absolutely. It may not happen as quickly or with such stunning rewards, but the situation can turn around!

Establishing Christ's Presence in Your World

Get alone or with other believers who are your friends. Pray about the negative situation you are facing. If the problem is massively pervasive in culture, pray about a specific display of that problem in your school or your city. Pray until you get God's directives. Pray specifically for each person you know is contributing to the problem or may be behind it. Ask for God to give you the insights you need and the response you should make.

Take a positive step, trusting God to work in ways only God can work.

Reflect or Discuss

- Why do people allow themselves to continue to be bullied for months, even years? What needs to be healed in those who accept bullying without challenging it?

Don't be passive in the face of bullying.
Activate the power of prayer!

CHAPTER TEN

You Can Ask for God's Help with Boldness

Daniel didn't seem to have much trouble in speaking up or acting in a bold manner. This may have been because he was still a teenager or young man in his early twenties when many of the stories in the book of Daniel took place. Teenagers often don't have any trouble speaking their minds!

You do not have, because you do not ask God.
(JAMES 4:2)

Daniel's boldness may have been the result of his concluding at the time of his captivity, *Everything has been taken from me except my life, and losing my life might not be such a bad thing.* When a person truly confronts his own mortality and concludes that there are things far worse than death, a certain boldness seems to take root in a person's soul. Certainly for the Christian, there is nothing more glo-

rious than death because it means being in the near presence of the Lord forever. I'm not at all saying we should desire to die, but we should not fear death. It is a transition for the Christian directly into God's presence.

The boldness of this young Hebrew man may have been a result of a maturity that was beyond his years, perhaps as the result of his captivity and his conquest of the king's intense training program. The more mature a person becomes, the more that person seems to adopt the attitude that says, *I have very little to lose and a great deal to gain by speaking up and taking a stand.*

We don't know why Daniel was so bold. What we do know is that many people around us today are not bold!

Some people seem to conclude that timidity is part of their personalities. I don't see any place in God's Word, however, where timidity was considered a good character trait. In many of the most famous Bible stories, God seemed to push and prod His heroes to move beyond their timidity! Moses seemed reluctant to head back to Egypt to confront Pharaoh, but God required this of him. Gideon may have been timid, but God called him to take very bold action. Saul was hiding out among the luggage carts when the Lord used Samuel to call him into a position of leadership as Israel's first king.

The apostle Paul wrote to Timothy, "God did not give us a spirit of timidity." Therefore, Paul said, "fan into flame the gift of God" (2 Tim. 1:7, 6).

Fan into Flame a Spirit of Boldness

How can we overcome the timidity we feel in a troublesome situation?

HAVE GODLY MOTIVES AND A CLEAR CONSCIENCE

First, we must know with certainty that we are acting out of a clear conscience. We must be sure we are not seeking to manipulate

others or to exert our personal power over them but are seeking
their good.

When the apostle Paul was brought before the religious rulers in
Jerusalem, the first words out of his mouth were these: "My brothers, I have fulfilled my duty to God in all good conscience to this
day" (Acts 23:1). When he spoke before Felix, Paul boldly said, "I
admit that I worship the God of our fathers as a follower of the
Way. . . . So I strive always to keep my conscience clear before God
and man" (Acts 24:14, 16).

Check your motives for speaking or acting. What do you really
hope to accomplish?

Is your goal of benefit to other people, or just yourself?

Is your purpose to draw attention to yourself, or to a problem
that needs to be solved?

Is your motivation to become the leader of an organization—
and be paid handsomely for your leadership—or to be a servant to
people who genuinely are in need, danger, or are living without due
justice?

Certainly you may end up receiving personal benefit from what
you say or do in seeking to right a wrong or solve a problem. You
may be one of the plaintiffs, victims, or codefendants in a situation.
You may end up on the front page of the newspaper, be tapped to
lead a group, or be rewarded for what you do. *But* . . . your innermost motivation must be pure before God. You must have a clear
conscience that you truly are acting for the good of the whole, and
not for selfish purposes.

James was very clear on this point: "When you ask, you do not
receive, because you ask with wrong motives, that you may spend
what you get on your pleasures" (James 4:3).

When Daniel went to Nebuchadnezzar to tell the king what he
had dreamed and what the dream meant, he went out of concern
not only for his own life, but for the lives of his friends and all the
wise men in Babylon. He didn't go seeking a higher position of
authority, fame, or material goods. Those things were given to

him, but they were not his motivation in going to the king with boldness.

DISCERN GOD'S CALL TO ACTION

Second, we must know with certainty that we are carrying out what we believe God desires for us to do. This certainty may come from something you read in the Bible, something you hear preached in a sermon by a godly minister, or as the result of a deep inner conviction, vision, or call of God that is abiding, intense, and something you cannot sidestep. If there is a burning in your soul to take a specific action, a deep, convicting spirit that you know is from God, that's a very strong signal that God is requiring you to speak up or take action. When Paul spoke before Festus and King Agrippa, he said, "I was not disobedient to the vision from heaven. . . . I have had God's help to this very day" (Acts 26:19, 22).

HAVE A GODLY ATTITUDE IN ASKING

Daniel first went to Nebuchadnezzar to ask for time. He didn't demand it. He requested it. Furthermore, he asked for time "so that he might interpret the dream for him" (Dan. 2:16). Daniel was seeking to do something good for the king. His attitude and approach were godly.

Are you seeking justice, retribution, a solution, an answer, or resolution of a conflict with the right attitude? Are you acting out of anger, rebellion, greed, or a desire to get your own way? If so, God isn't likely to honor your boldness!

Go to those who have the ability to help you meet a need with kindness, reasonable and gentle words, and a desire to help the person in authority to be a better, more respected, and more effective leader.

When one of the godliest women in the Old Testament, Abigail, went to David to take him a gift from her home, she knew that her life, along with the lives of her entire household, was in danger. Abigail's husband, Nabal, had affronted David by not sharing the sheep-shearing feast with David and his men, who had provided security for some of Nabal's shepherds. Abigail didn't demand that David accept her gift. Rather, she got off her donkey, bowed down before David with her face to the ground, and said, "Please let your servant speak to you" (1 Sam. 25:24).

Abigail went on to appeal to David's leadership, calling him "master." She said,

> Please forgive your servant's offense, for the LORD will certainly make a lasting dynasty for my master, because he fights the LORD's battles. . . . When the LORD has done for my master every good thing he promised concerning him and has appointed him leader over Israel, my master will not have on his conscience the staggering burden of needless bloodshed or of having avenged himself. (1 Samuel 25:28, 30–31)

David responded favorably to Abigail and reversed his decision to wipe out Nabal and all of his household. Abigail's life was spared, but not hers alone. She went with a godly attitude and prevailed in securing the safety of all she loved.

James said this about our attitude in asking: "You want something but don't get it. You kill and covet, but you cannot have what you want. You quarrel and fight" (James 4:2). These are the wrong ways to use boldness! These attitudes reflect a form of pride — they are the attitudes of those who believe they deserve to have what they want, and they demand from others rather than ask. The Bible tells us clearly that "God opposes the proud but gives grace to the humble" (James 4:6; see Prov. 3:34).

Go with a humble attitude. That does not make you any less bold. It just makes you more effective.

Ask God for an Infusion of Courage

A person came to me not long ago after I had preached on boldness and said, "I have wished for many years to be bolder, but I never thought to ask God for boldness. I thought it was something I totally had to muster up on my own. I never saw it as something God might give to me or plant in me. I'm going home and get on my knees and ask for a massive *infusion* of boldness!"

I like that phrase, "infusion of boldness." More of us need one!

The Bible tells us, "You do not have, because you do not ask God" (James 4:2). It is God's pleasure to give you those things that are in line with heaven's will for every believer in Christ Jesus, and boldness is one of those things that is squarely in heaven's will!

Jesus had a great deal to say about our need for asking before we receive:

> Ask and it will be given to you; seek and you will find; knock and the door will be opened to you. For everyone who asks receives; he who seeks finds; and to him who knocks, the door will be opened. Which of you, if his son asks for bread, will give him a stone? Or if he asks for a fish, will give him a snake? If you, then, though you are evil, know how to give good gifts to your children, how much more will your Father in heaven give good gifts to those who ask him! (Matthew 7:7–11)

> I will do whatever you ask in my name, so that the Son may bring glory to the Father. You may ask me for anything in my name, and I will do it. (John 14:13–14)

> If you believe, you will receive whatever you ask for in prayer. (Matthew 21:22)

Believe today that if you ask God for an infusion of boldness, He will give you such an infusion.

And then, don't be surprised if God gives you even more boldness than you ever thought imaginable! Countless people have said after they spoke up for the truth or acted in a bold way to bring about the establishment of God's justice, "I surprised even myself."

Maybe so. But I doubt God was surprised, and I feel sure God was pleased! God's Word assures us, "Now to him who is able to do immeasurably more than all we ask or imagine, according to his power that is at work within us, to him be glory in the church and in Christ Jesus throughout all generations, for ever and ever!" (Eph. 3:20–21).

The infusion of boldness that God gives to those who ask for it is an infusion of His power, intended to bring Him glory. To ask for an infusion of boldness is simply to say, "God, use me in the ways You desire to use me. Don't let my timidity stand in the way. Give me courage. Give me strength. Give me wisdom. And help me to act boldly today!"

Establishing Christ's Presence in Your World

Get on your knees before God and ask Him to purify your motives, fill you with kindness, and make very clear what He desires for you to say or do. Ask Him for an infusion of boldness.

Reflect or Discuss

- What keeps us from asking God for the good things He desires to give? Are we afraid that our loving heavenly Father might say no? How does that line up with the whole of God's Word on asking and receiving?

Be bold in asking God for boldness!

CHAPTER ELEVEN

You Can Face Life's Tests Head-On

Life is filled with tests. I'm not talking about the kind that teachers give in schools. I'm talking about the kind that challenge your opinions, call upon you to defend your actions, require that you say no to evil, and compel you to speak up or take action even if it means you might be criticized or ridiculed.

The Lord knows how to rescue godly men from trials and to hold the unrighteous for the day of judgment.

(2 PETER 2:9)

Life's tests rarely come when we feel strong enough to handle them or are fully prepared to answer them. Most of life's tests are pop quizzes. They come when we least expect them and often feel weak and unprepared to pass them.

Such a test came to Daniel's friends Hananiah, Mishael, and Azariah, who by this time were known in Babylon by both the Israelites and the Babylonians

as Shadrach, Meshach, and Abednego. The test came out of the blue.

One of the most powerful evidences of the power of one is how those whom they influence can multiply themselves. In this chapter we will see the power of one multiplied as Daniel's followers imitated him and took a stand.

Nebuchadnezzar had authorized the construction of a giant monument to himself and his reign. An image of gold was set up in Dura in the Babylon province—it was ninety feet high and nine feet wide. This nine-story pillar most likely was visible from every corner of the city.

After the monument was completed, Nebuchadnezzar summoned all of the leaders to come to a dedication of the image. As the "satraps, prefects, governors, advisers, treasurers, judges, magistrates, and all the other provincial officials" stood before the monument, a herald announced,

> This is what you are commanded to do, O peoples, nations and men of every language: As soon as you hear the sound of the horn, flute, zither, lyre, harp, pipes and all kinds of music, you must fall down and worship the image of gold that King Nebuchadnezzar has set up. Whoever does not fall down and worship will immediately be thrown into a blazing furnace. (Daniel 3:2, 4–6)

It was a test—a simple but highly consequential pass/fail test!

The Nature of the Test

The rules of the test were very clear.

First, nobody was exempt. There was no provision for excuses.

Second, the behavior required was very explicit: the leaders were to prostrate themselves before the monument and worship it. This act of falling facedown into the sand before the image was a sign of complete obedience to the rule and power of Nebuchadnezzar and the Babylonian authority that he represented. Some of the men gathered on the plain were from other cultures and nations, including the Hebrew leaders of the province, Shadrach, Meshach, and Abednego. To bow is to affirm: "There is no power higher than Nebuchadnezzar. I give him my complete homage and obedience."

Third, the signal for worshiping was universal so there could be no misunderstanding based upon languages—the language of music was to be the signal for prostration. Perhaps a special song was composed just for this event. Perhaps the music was something like the national anthem of Babylon. It appears that a full orchestra was assembled, with the capability of sending a message of music a significant distance.

Fourth, the penalty for failing to pass the test would be immediate death by fire. It is interesting that this was to be the means of death. Throughout the ancient pagan world, sacrifices to false gods were often made by fire. Some of the pagan peoples even burned their children as sacrifices. Nebuchadnezzar was saying, in effect, "Bow or burn—either way, you will be making a sacrifice to this image." By adding the fire sacrifice to the ceremony, Nebuchadnezzar was making this monument not only a national symbol of Babylon, but an idol, a false god. He was moving himself from being an earthly king to being a deity. He was requiring on behalf of himself something that was normally required only by the "gods."

The test was a test of life-and-death commitment. Are you aware that every day you face similar tests—perhaps not quite so obvious, but just as real?

Temptation vs. Test

In the Bible, a test is usually described as a temptation. A temptation is a test of our value system and our resolve to serve God. God does not tempt His people with sin. The Bible is very clear on that point:

When tempted, no one should say, "God is tempting me." For God cannot be tempted by evil, nor does he tempt anyone; but each one is tempted when, by his own evil desire, he is dragged away and enticed. Then, after desire has conceived, it gives birth to sin; and sin, when it is full-grown, gives birth to death. (James 1:13–15)

The devil, who is called the "tempter," presents to every person tests that he believes that person will fail! His temptations are intended to entice us into sin, which will steal the potential for God's blessing, kill our reputation, and if pursued to its final outcome, cause us to die. He presents his temptations not only as enticements for forbidden pleasure, but also as trials and difficulties that cause us to doubt the goodness and love of God.

From the devil's perspective, a temptation is a stumbling block — an obstacle thrown into the path of life to trip you up and cause you to fall into sinful habits, deep failure, a bad reputation, or evil company, or any other negative outcome.

But — and thank God there is another side to this coin — from God's perspective, a temptation from the devil is a test of our faith to reveal to us the power that comes when we rely upon God to help us say no to temptation. God's Word holds out a wonderful sequence of positive outcomes associated with overcoming temptation. James 1:2–4 tells us, "Consider it pure joy, my brothers, whenever you face trials of many kinds, because you know that the testing of your faith develops perseverance. Perseverance must finish its work so that you may be mature and complete, not lacking anything." James goes on to say, "Blessed is the man who perseveres under trial, because when he has stood the test, he will receive the crown of life that God has promised to those who love him" (James 1:12).

The end result of overcoming a temptation is *all good*. When we overcome temptation we become more mature, more fulfilled, more prepared for greater success and service, and in the end, we become the recipients of great heavenly rewards.

What the devil intends as a stumbling stone, God uses as a building block!

The devil was using Nebuchadnezzar to tempt the officials of Babylon, including Shadrach, Meshach, and Abednego.

God had a plan for turning that temptation into a tremendous blessing for those who would pass the test.

The Tests of Our Culture

How does this test of Nebuchadnezzar relate to us? There are at least four ways.

1. NO ONE IS IMMUNE TO TEMPTATION

First, no one today is immune to the pervasive temptations of our culture to engage in sin. You cannot drive down a street or highway, turn on a radio or television set, pass by a magazine rack, or enter a movie theater without facing messages that are designed to lure you one step closer to sin. You may not have any intention of sinning, or of reading, viewing, or participating in what you see advertised or portrayed, but you nonetheless are going to be exposed to temptation. It doesn't matter how long you've been a Christian or how immune you think you are because of the depth of your commitment to Christ Jesus—you can and will be tempted from time to time. There is no vaccination for temptation.

2. FALSE GODS AND IDOLS ARE PREVALENT

Second, temptations abound at every turn to worship a false god. We may not think we are surrounded by idols, but that's because we have an incorrect perception about what an idol really is. An idol is anything in which a person puts his trust.

Some people think that an idol is something that we trust more than we trust God. The true definition of *idol* according to the Bible is anything that we trust for our security, provision, or fulfillment. When God commanded the Israelites, "You shall have no other gods before Me," He was also saying, "When I look out over the camp of the Israelites, I don't want to see any gods before My eyes. I don't want to see them hidden in your tents or garments. I don't want you trusting in anything or anyone other than Me for your security, provision, or fulfillment as a people."

Whom or what are you trusting today for your income? For your retirement?

Whom or what are you trusting today for your happiness? For your sense of fulfillment and purpose?

Whom or what are you trusting today for your health?

Whom or what are you trusting today for your identity? A spouse? A career? A child or grandchild?

Trust is a very big issue to God. He said through His prophet Zephaniah that He would destroy all those who trusted in anything but Him and save a remnant of people who were the "meek and humble, / who trust in the name of the LORD" (Zeph. 3:12).

We may not think we are being asked to worship an idol, but that's because we have an incorrect definition for *worship*. To worship is to serve. Worship is an act of obedience in doing what God requires of us. When a person worships a false god or an idol, that person begins to serve the idol by doing what is required to maintain the idol.

Consider the person who has a home at the lake that he can visit on weekends. That home needs maintenance — so does the boat at the dock. When does he do that maintenance? Often on Sunday mornings. Who or what is he serving on Sunday mornings? God or the house and boat at the lake?

Consider the person who is committed to filling an IRA account for retirement. That is what the person is trusting for adequate funds in old age. How is that IRA served? By automatic withdrawals from a paycheck, sometimes before the automatic withdrawals for tax and Social Security from the same paycheck. But let anybody suggest automatic withdrawals for tithes and offerings, and you won't hear the end of the uproar! Who or what are you serving in the management of your finances?

Consider the person who is committed to working out every day. The person is trusting physical fitness to keep him alive longer and in better health. He goes faithfully to the gym every night after work. His fitness level needs daily servicing. But what happens when he comes home from the gym on Wednesday evening? Is he too tired to go to Bible study or prayer meeting? Whom or what is he serving?

No one is immune to the temptation of a false god or idol.

No one is immune to the temptation to worship that idol.

3. THE UNIVERSAL NATURE OF TEMPTATION

Third, we also need to recognize that the messages of temptation have become universal. The average person today in the United States and other westernized nations wouldn't dream of living without a television set, a computer, or a cell phone. Most people wouldn't dream of doing without fast foods and fast automobiles. The products and technology of our world are universal. You're going to find television sets in the most remote regions of the world, right next to the soft-drink machine, and near the marketplace stall that sells minutes on cell phones!

A woman told me one time about an experience she had in a suburb of Paris. She said, "I don't speak French but when I walked into this little mall, I was surprised to see the names of some of the most famous clothing designers in the world. In the shop windows I saw the same sign again and again. I don't read French, but I knew immediately what that sign said because it was in nearly every window. The sign said, 'Sale'!"

We have a universal understanding in our world of buy, sell, use, take. We also have an understanding that is rooted in what people consider to be their "rights," some of which are not true rights but what they wish could be their rights. We have an understanding of the words *easy*, *cheap*, *on sale*, and *available*. We have a universal understanding of the words *demand* and *terrorism*.

It's as if the whole world is marching to a tune that says, "You can have what you want, right now, with virtually no effort or responsibility, if you will just *take* what you want by any means possible." This message is founded, of course, on the notion that you can know what is best for you.

God's Word presents an entirely different message. It declares, "You must seek first the kingdom of God." It takes effort, discipline, and faith to say no to evil and yes to what is good. A love for God and a love for others are necessary if you truly are going to have what matters most in this life and in the next life. Mankind doesn't know what is best—God does.

Don't be tricked by the universality of the message. Just because everybody is doing it, buying it, using it, or pursuing it doesn't make it worthy of having or doing! Jesus said, "Enter through the narrow gate. For wide is the gate and broad is the road that leads to destruction, and many enter through it. But small is the gate and narrow the road that leads to life, and only a few find it" (Matt. 7:13–14).

4. THE DEADLY CONSEQUENCES OF SIN

Fourth, the devil is rarely as straightforward as Nebuchadnezzar was. He doesn't tell you, "Do this or die." He also doesn't reveal that if you do certain things, and you do them habitually, you will die. The devil is usually much more subtle. The word *deceive* means "to trick or to mislead."

The devil says, "It isn't a sin," even if God says it is.

The devil says, "You have a misunderstanding of what's real and what's good," even if God clearly spells out what's real and what's good.

The devil says, "You won't be harmed," even if God says the results of sin are deadly (Rom. 3:23).

Rather than tell a person the full consequences or nature of sin, the devil holds out the terrible consequences that will occur if a person doesn't yield to temptation. He usually presents to a person this lie: "If you don't fulfill your own lusts and passions . . . if you don't buy into the cultural norms . . . if you don't run the rat race to success with all your energy and effort . . . you will be left out, left behind, or left holding the bag for somebody else. You will be unhappy and filled with frustration. You may just burn up in your own desires for a better life, more sex, more fame, more money, and more happiness. It's far better to bow to the norms of the culture than to go down in the flames of your own individuality and stance for doing the right thing."

That's the temptation.

That's the lie.

And that's the opportunity for advancement of your faith.

Resist—with Resolute Strength

When I was in my early twenties, I found myself in an environment that was very hostile to all of the principles and values that I held to be true and important. I was tempted again and again to compromise in my beliefs and behavior.

The only way I knew to respond to negative pressure in my work environment was to say no and to say it repeatedly and with conviction. I said no so many times in such a short period of time that people around me began to say when they heard a definitive, conclusive, strong no, "That's a Youssef no!" I meant what I said and nobody had any doubts about it.

Shadrach, Meshach, and Abednego said no, actually without saying a word.

The king said, "Bow."

They remained standing.

All around them, people bowed.

They remained standing.

The music blared.

They remained standing.

The fiery furnace sizzled and roared.

They remained standing.

Shadrach, Meshach, and Abednego had seen their friend and leader stand strong in faith before the king. Even without Daniel present, they followed his example.

When you are tempted to serve false idols, say no. Say it every time. Say it with conviction. Sometimes the power of one is displayed as a quiet determination to stand strong, even when the vast majority is caving in.

Establishing Christ's Presence in Your World

Identify at least one temptation that seems to surface again and again in your life. What do you need to do to shut the door on that temptation? Do you need to change your shopping habits, your reading habits, your viewing habits? Do you need to make adjustments in how you spend your time or your money? Do you need to sell something, cancel something, resign from something, or let something go? Do you need to make a change in friends, stop going certain places, or stop participating in certain activities? Ask God to help you shut the door on temptation and open the door to full obedience.

Consider asking someone you trust to be an accountability partner to you in saying no to a recurring temptation in your life.

Reflect or Discuss

- How difficult is it to say no to something that everybody else is saying yes to? What gives a person the courage to say no to temptation? How might you build safeguards into your life to help you withstand temptation?

Determine in your heart that your answer to God will always be *Yes* and your answer to the devil will always be a resounding *No!*

CHAPTER TWELVE

You Can Appeal to Higher Authority

From the time we are little children we are told that it is wrong to be a tattletale, that it isn't good to "squeal" on other people who are doing wrong. We are taught that if you can't say something nice about another person, you shouldn't say anything at all.

Were we given good advice?

Maybe not.

The Bible presents a balance between turning the other cheek when we are ridiculed and confronting those who say that what we do is wrong and what we say is a lie. We need to be very wise in deciding when to take action, and when not to. And then, we need to be very wise in discerning to whom we should appeal for help.

Let us then approach the throne of grace with confidence, so that we may receive mercy and find grace to help us in our time of need.

(HEBREWS 4:16)

Turn the Other Cheek or Defend Your Position?

Jesus taught this to His followers, "You have heard that it was said, 'Eye for eye, and tooth for tooth.' But I tell you, Do not resist an evil person. If someone strikes you on the right cheek, turn to him the other also" (Matt. 5:38–39).

Jesus was confronting the spirit of revenge in this teaching. Certainly we see a spirit of revenge operating in full force all around us today. There's a deep cycle of revenge in all the nations of the Middle East. There is also a deep cycle of revenge and retaliation in many political circles, and a cycle of lash and backlash between the rich and poor, blacks and whites, and the haves and have-nots in our society. Nothing can stop a cycle of revenge except the forgiveness of God settling deep in the hearts of those who are on both sides of every fence.

To strike a person on the cheek was a sign of scorn in Bible times. It was a signal that the person being struck was offensive or insulting in some way. Job wrote that when he was covered with boils and sitting in misery, his opponents would "strike [his] cheek in scorn" (Job 16:10). Job's enemies ridiculed him for refusing to believe he had brought his suffering down on himself because of sin.

As I mentioned earlier, I spent more than eight years in Australia and I learned some of the terms and phrases they use. They are fond of using the word *cheeky* to describe a person who is rude or disrespectful. The word implies that a person deserves to have his or her cheek slapped. In old classic films, when a man tried to steal a kiss from a woman, he was considered to be acting in a cheeky manner — and often in those old films the man did get his cheek slapped!

If people are criticizing or rejecting you, or in any other way putting you down because of who you are and what you stand for as a Christian, so be it. It's not your fault that they can't bear to hear the truth from you and are insulted by your words or behavior. Take what they dish out and don't respond in kind. If they call you names, refuse to call them names in return. If they write horrible things about you, refuse to write horrible things in return. If you respond, you will only be creating a cycle of revenge that can become crueler and crueler.

Although the sting of a strike on the cheek may be painful, if it's a strike against you for speaking the truth and the person feeling insulted by the truth, that slap on the cheek is something of a compliment. It says that your words struck a chord deep within the person.

On the other hand . . . God does not call us to stay silent when people try to twist the truth of what we say into a lie. We are not to keep quiet when people accuse us of lying about the truth of God's Word or accuse us of politically incorrect behavior when we have acted in obedience to God's Word.

This is happening more and more in our culture as people call Christians "intolerant," "unloving," "fanatical," and even "silly" or "stupid."

It's one thing to take personal insults. It's another thing to stay silent when someone blatantly misinterprets as wrong your behavior that is in keeping with God's commandments. The only sin the world seems to recognize today is the sin of intolerance. It is not intolerant to speak what is right, true, and good even as you tolerate a person's right to call you names. You need to respond, "God has a tremendous amount of patience with sinners, but no tolerance for sin. God's Word presents absolutes about right and wrong and we are told to be good evaluators about what is right and wrong behavior. God's Word tells me I must love the sinner and hate the sin. That's not intolerance — that is a fact." I am convinced that when you love a sinner and hate the sin, sooner or later it will make an impact on some.

Don't Let a Lie Go Unchallenged

Don't allow the lies of others to stick to you because you fail to openly reject the lie. We are wise to absorb personal insults, but not lies.

Don't let unbelievers define the terms of your faith! Know what you believe and why.

Do you have a good definition for salvation? Do you know why a person needs salvation?

Do you have a good definition for words such as *righteousness, redemption, sanctification,* or *justification*? Those are five-dollar Bible words to many people, but the concepts they convey are vitally important for you to understand if you are a Christian. (We'll be discussing them later in this book.)

Just as you don't let unbelievers define your faith, you must not let them ascribe to you attitudes or motives that you do not have.

It is not unloving to confront a person in his or her sin even as you point the way toward forgiveness of that sin. In truth, it's the most *loving* thing you can do for a person to say with great compassion, "God desires for you to be set free from that sin."

It's not "fanatical" to be a Christian. That's the foundation for our nation and our rule of law. We must not stand idly by and allow *Christian* to be equated with aberrant or insane!

It's not "silly" or "stupid" to believe the Scriptures and to apply them to daily life. It's *wisdom*! What is truly foolish is for disobedient people to turn a blind eye to the truth of a sign that says "Cliff Ahead" and proceed to walk off the cliff!

What Must You Refute?

The Lord spoke to His people through the prophet Isaiah, saying, "No weapon forged against you will prevail, / and you will refute every tongue that accuses you. / This is the heritage of the servants of the LORD" (Isa. 54:17).

Christians are often quick to quote, "No weapon forged against you will prevail." They are far more reluctant to "refute every tongue that accuses you." What does it mean to do this?

It means, first and foremost, that when people tell you that your judgment in a matter is incorrect—that you are lying or that your stand for absolutes is wrong—you continue to respond in boldness, saying, "I am speaking the truth of God's Word." When people tell you that your assessment of a situation is wrong, you quickly respond, "My assessment is accurate according to God's Word." Then open up your Bible and let them read aloud God's Word for themselves.

If you are planning to confront a person about a lie he or she is telling about you or what you believe, make sure you are prepared! Look up the truth of God's Word so that you can quickly turn to passages that address the issue at hand.

Make Certain You Don't Deserve the Persecution

We must be very clear on one point: we can't complain if we deserve the slap on the cheek. If we are acting in an unkind or disrespectful way, we have no grounds on which to say that we have been treated badly. If we misquote God's Word or use it in a self-serving, manipulative way, we have no grounds on which to defend ourselves.

Make very certain that when you speak up for the truth and take action to right a wrong that you do so in a polite and courteous way, with strength of conviction and the Word of God clearly on your side!

To Whom Should You Appeal?

When you know that you need to speak up in order to refute a lie, also know to whom you should speak and appeal for help.

In the case of Shadrach, Meshach, and Abednego, as they confronted an order to bow in worship before a massive nine-story idol Nebuchadnezzar erected, they had no one to whom they could appeal but God.

At other times in the Scriptures, people were very wise to appeal to those in authority who might help them.

When Esther learned that a close adviser to her husband, a wicked man named Haman, was plotting to destroy her and all her people, she made a plan to appeal to her husband, King Xerxes. It was a bold move on Esther's part. Even her approaching the king without being summoned held the potential for a death sentence or his dismissing her as his queen. Nevertheless, Esther asked her cousin to lead people in fasting and praying on her behalf and she prepared herself to entertain the king and confront him with Haman's plot. She succeeded.

When Paul was accused falsely and arrested in Jerusalem for supposedly starting a riot, Paul appealed to higher and higher authorities, finally to Caesar. As a Roman citizen, he had the right to that level of justice, and he pursued it.

To whom might you appeal for help in attaining justice for those who are being treated unfairly or unjustly?

To whom might you go with information about a plot that you believe is about to be launched against you, your community, or your nation?

From whom might you request assistance in confronting the behavior of an abuser or a criminal?

Ask God to give you guidance. Fast and pray until you know clearly that you are pursuing an appeal to the right person, at the right time, and that you are going to that person with the right spirit.

Confront the behavior.

Confront the lie.

Do so in a way that does not result in an exchange of name-calling or empty accusations. Stay focused on the wrong behavior, the sinful action, the lying statements. God raises people to positions of authority so they can get things done. We must pray for our leaders that they will get the *right* things done. We must be bold in stating to them what we believe the right things are.

Establishing Christ's Presence in Your World

Identify at least one lie that you believe needs to be challenged. Has that lie been associated with you personally, or has it been linked to a group to which you belong? If the lie is linked to a group, get with others from the group. Discuss how you can and should challenge the lie. Ask God to show you what to say to the person who is accusing you, how to speak, and when to speak.

Reflect or Discuss

- What criteria can you use to determine if something is a personal insult against you or is a genuine lie about the truth of God that you have stated?
- How might we confront lies without resorting to anger or insults of our own against another person?

Take a personal insult, but challenge lies.

CHAPTER THIRTEEN

You Can Experience God's Presence with You

Very few people have known the presence of God as did King David. He longed for the presence of God and found his greatest delight in the refuge of God Himself. Throughout the Psalms we discover that David considered the presence of God to be the ultimate dwelling place. He wrote:

> *You have made known to me*
> *the path of life;*
> *you will fill me with joy in*
> *your presence,*
> *with eternal pleasures at your*
> *right hand.*
>
> (PSALM 16:11)

How great is your goodness,
    which you have stored up for those
    who fear you,
which you bestow in the sight of men
    on those who take refuge in you.
In the shelter of your presence
    you hide them from the intrigues of
    men;
in your dwelling you keep them safe
    from accusing tongues.

(PSALM 31:19–20)

The psalmist longed for God's presence. Like a deer "pants for streams of water," his soul thirsted for God (Ps. 42:1).

God's presence throughout the Bible is associated with strength. He is a strong tower, a refuge in time of trouble, a mighty fortress that shields and protects from enemy assault. To know the presence of God is to feel safe and secure.

Daniel's protégés, Shadrach, Meshach, and Abednego, learned from his power of one to experience God in even the most difficult hour of their lives. They experienced it in the midst of a burning furnace. This was a furnace in which the heat was not only so intense that it burned immediately, but it was a fiery furnace with flames dancing wildly within. What a place to experience God!

Some time ago, a woman told me about a conversation she had as a child with her grandmother. She was spending the night at her grandmother's home and her grandmother had suggested that she read her Bible and pray before going to bed. The girl asked, "How long should I read? How long should I pray?"

Her grandmother responded in a profound way. She said:

- You should read your Bible until you read something that really applies to you. In that moment, you will have heard the voice of God in your spirit.
- You should pray until you weep for your own sins and the souls of others you love. When you do that, you will experience the love of God—you will know how much He loves you, even as you know how much He loves other people.
- You should praise God until you are assured that He is bigger than all of your problems and greater than all your accomplishments. When you do that, you will have confidence that God's strong arms are upholding you.
- You should cry out to God when you have problems until you experience His peace. That's God's Spirit surrounding you and shielding you.

"She said all that?" I asked.

"Yes," the woman said. "My grandmother told me that she had been taught these lines by her grandmother and she had memorized them as a child. I was so impressed by what she said that I asked her to help me memorize them too."

Then the woman concluded with a tear in her eye, "I have never forgotten what Grandma said. She taught me that night how to know God."

That grandmother had it right! She knew the keys to experiencing God's presence in a life-changing and empowering way. Any time a person puts himself in a position to hear the voice of God, feel the love of God, experience the peace of God, and be aware of the strength of God, that person has entered into God's intimate presence.

Long Before the Furnace

Relationships take time to build. You don't enter into the depths and heights of knowing God or experiencing His presence in the first moment of your relationship with Him. The time to develop an intimate relationship with God is long before a crisis hits.

Shadrach, Meshach, and Abednego didn't have the privilege of stopping Nebuchadnezzar's ceremony to hold a prayer meeting. When the music started playing, they had an instant decision to make: bow or stay standing.

There's an interesting difference between the positions of prayer the pagan people used and those of God's people in the ancient world. The pagan position for worship was to bow low, face in the dirt. The pagan peoples did this in deference to their gods and their leaders. The Jewish position of prayer and worship was standing, with arms raised from the elbow up and palms open and facing outward. This was the position of the high priest in the temple as he stood facing the Holy of Holies each day. It was a position of respect, nothing being withheld from God and nothing being claimed as one's own. A person standing before God in prayer with open and raised palms was saying, in effect, "Examine me, Lord. See that I'm keeping nothing back from You and that I'm relying on You to give me everything I need or will ever have. I want You to know me thoroughly, even as I desire to know You."

The Jewish position for prayer also expressed an understanding of the way God had dealt with those He had chosen for centuries as the leaders of the Israelites. They were never asked to grovel. Rather, they were invited to come before God in humility and respect, but in a relationship that was marked by direct communication.

When Shadrach, Meshach, and Abednego chose to remain standing, they sent a very strong body-language signal. They immediately put themselves in the prayer position of the Hebrew people standing in the presence of Jehovah God, not in the prayer position of the Babylonians groveling before pagan gods. In their spirits, I have no doubt they were crying out to God, even though they didn't utter a word.

Crying Out to God

Throughout the Bible, and especially in the Psalms, God's people cried out to Him for help, sustenance, deliverance, and strength. Let me share with you just a few examples:

> I call to God,
>   and the LORD saves me.
> Evening, morning, and noon
>   I cry out in distress,
>   and he hears my voice.
> He ransoms me unharmed
>   from the battle waged against me,
>   even though many oppose me.
>
> (PSALM 55:16–18)

> I love the LORD, for he heard my voice;
>   he heard my cry for mercy.

Because he turned his ear to me,
   I will call on him as long as I live.
(PSALM 116:1–2)

They cried to the LORD in their trouble,
   and he saved them from their distress.
(PSALM 107:19)

When they cry to the LORD because of their oppressors, he
will send them a savior and defender, and he will rescue them.
(ISAIAH 19:20)

To cry before the Lord means to come before Him in complete vulnerability. There's no holding back, no putting on a brave face, and no attempt to negotiate. To cry before the Lord means to cast your entire self upon the Lord because you know from the very core of your being that you cannot survive without God. It is to come to God with extreme humility and dependence, willing to express every emotion with abandon.

The truth is, God knows how you feel. When you cry to the Lord, *you* have a full realization of how you feel! You know that God knows and you know that God knows that you know. It's a case of: "I know that You know that I know that You know."

A person who is crying out to God is desperate for answers, and he's not proud, thinking he can come up with those answers by himself. He knows he is utterly dependent upon God to provide what is missing.

To cry out to God is to rush to Him and shout "Help!" rather than casually stroll toward the throne of God and say, "Oh, by the way, Lord, there's a little situation over here that I think You might want to take a look at. Perhaps You can do something about it."

You can cry to the Lord in your heart, even if no noise comes out of your mouth. To cry before the Lord is first and foremost an attitude in your spirit. It is a feeling of total dependence.

Of one thing we can be certain: God hears and answers the cry of the heart. He immediately moves to fill what is missing in the person's life with His presence.

The person who cries out to God for mercy . . . feels God's forgiveness flooding into his life.

The person who cries out to God for help in times of fear and anxiety . . . feels God's peace filling his heart and mind.

The person who cries out to God in loneliness or in anguish at a loss . . . feels God's comforting and abiding friendship.

God always answers the deepest cries of our heart *first* with His own presence, and then in practical ways. He assures us that He is with us, He is for us, and He will act on our behalf, and *then* He takes on our enemies and our needs.

Shadrach, Meshach, and Abednego knew this to be true. They had a strong awareness that God was with them and that God was honoring what they did, even if God should choose to do nothing about the furnace.

What happened when the music sounded and everybody bowed except these three Hebrew men? Well, it was obvious that they were still standing. The Chaldean astrologers were only too quick to point that out. They said to the king, "There are some Jews whom you have set over the affairs of the province of Babylon — Shadrach, Meshach and Abednego — who pay no attention to you, O king. They neither serve your gods nor worship the image of gold you have set up" (Dan. 3:12).

Nebuchadnezzar was "furious with rage." He summoned them and said, "Is is true?" These were men who had Nebuchadnezzar's respect and admiration. He no doubt was stunned at this seeming act of rebellion. He gave them another chance, adding, "What god will be able to rescue you from my hand?" (Dan. 3:13, 14, 16).

Shadrach, Meshach, and Abednego — filled with the presence of God — replied,

> O Nebuchadnezzar, we do not need to defend ourselves before you in this matter. If we are thrown into the blazing

furnace, the God we serve is able to save us from it, and he will rescue us from your hand, O king. But even if he does not, we want you to know, O king, that we will not serve your gods or worship the image of gold you have set up. (Daniel 3:16–18)

The only thing hotter than Nebuchadnezzar's anger in that moment was the furnace. He ordered that it be heated seven times hotter and he commanded his strongest soldiers in the army to tie up the three men and throw them into the blaze. Shadrach, Meshach, and Abednego were thrown fully clothed into the furnace, which was so hot that the flames killed the soldiers who shoved them into it.

The place where you are thrown by life's circumstances or by someone who seeks to harm you may not be a furnace. You may be tossed into a prison cell . . . banned from speaking at an event . . . or tossed out on the street, fired from your company. You may be evicted from your home . . . disowned by your family . . . or divorced by your spouse. You may find yourself in bankruptcy court . . . the intensive care unit of a hospital . . . or isolated in a file room in the basement of the building.

Let me assure you of this: God sees you there. He hears the cry of your heart. And He is with you.

Acknowledge His presence.

Proclaim His love, power, and wisdom.

Thank Him in advance for delivering you.

Cling to Him as your Savior, Deliverer, Healer, Sustainer, and Provider.

And then, stand back and be prepared to watch your awesome God work on your behalf. Prepare to be amazed as He does what only He can do to receive the glory that only He deserves!

A Glory Brighter than the Heat of a Blazing Furnace

The heat of that furnace—even seven times hotter than normal— didn't faze these three bold ambassadors of the Most High God.

Nebuchadnezzar couldn't believe what he saw in the moments that followed their being thrown into the furnace, bound with ropes. Nebuchadnezzar leaped to his feat in amazement and said, "Weren't there three men that we tied up and threw into the fire?" The advisers close by replied, "Certainly, O king." He said, "Look! I see four men walking around in the fire, unbound and unharmed, and the fourth looks like a son of the gods" (Dan. 3:24–25).

A fiery furnace became a beautiful garden to Shadrach, Meshach, and Abednego. They strolled through those flames with praise and awe, experiencing the presence of God as never before! I can almost see them leaping about and dancing in the flames, darting in and out among them in unfettered exuberance. God, by the sheer force of His presence, had turned one of the most dastardly orders of all time into one of the most stunning miracles of the ages!

Nebuchadnezzar went to the opening of the furnace and shouted above the roar of the flames, "Shadrach, Meshach, and Abednego, servants of the Most High God, come out! Come here!" (Dan. 3:26).

Shadrach, Meshach, and Abednego strolled out of that furnace and I suspect they had huge grins on their faces. What the king had meant for their horror and suffering God had turned to their delight and joy. I think if I had been one of those young men I might have shouted back to the king, "I don't think I want to come out, king. Why don't you come in here and join me?" Shadrach, Meshach, and Abednego obeyed the king's command, however, and when they emerged from the fire, all those who had accused them and judged them could see that their bodies were not the least bit burned, not a hair on their heads was singed, and their robes weren't scorched. They didn't even smell like fire.

There's no situation in which you might be thrown today that is overwhelming to God. There's no situation that comes as a shocking surprise to God, or comes even close to being a circumstance that He can't handle. Not only is God with you in the crisis moment, upholding you by His very presence, but He can help you emerge from the situation unscathed. He has already planned His way through your problem. He knows the good ending He has for you, no matter how bad the beginning or how terrible the present moment.

Trust God to completely turn around the evil intended against you into a mighty triumph! That's what happened in the lives of these courageous young men. Nebuchadnezzar began to praise the God of Shadrach, Meshach, and Abednego. He said, "They trusted in him and defied the king's command and were willing to give up their lives rather than serve or worship any god except their own God." As a result, Nebuchadnezzar issued a decree that people who said anything against the God of Shadrach, Meshach, and Abednego were to be "cut into pieces and their houses be turned into piles of rubble" (Dan. 3:29). As for these three men, they each received a promotion!

The real monument that day on the plain of Dura was not a ninety-foot pillar erected in homage to Nebuchadnezzar and pagan gods. The real monument was a furnace filled with the glory of God—a glory that far outshone a blaze of flame. There are no archaeological remains of the image Nebuchadnezzar had erected in Babylon. What we do have is a lasting testament to God's power that has inspired faith and hope in God's people for thousands of years!

What made the difference in turning that king's fiery furnace into a dramatic stage for displaying God's deliverance power? The presence of God.

Nothing has greater power to change your circumstances.

Nothing has greater power to deliver you from evil.

Nothing has greater power to turn death from life and work all things to your good.

The presence of God makes the definitive difference in any situation, and in any life.

Establishing Christ's Presence in Your World

Read your Bible today until you read something that applies directly to your life. Pray today until you weep for your own sins and the needs of others.

Praise God today until you see God as being larger than any situation or problem in your life.

Cry out to God today to answer your deepest need until you feel His peace filling your heart.

Thank God for His presence with you. The King of the universe, Almighty and Ever-Living God, can and does indwell the lowly human heart that desires to know Him, worship Him, and is utterly dependent upon Him.

Reflect or Discuss

- Reflect upon an experience in your past in which you know that God, and God alone, delivered you from danger, death, or evil. What did you come to know about God from that experience? How did that experience change your life? How did it impact your faith?

Never lose sight of the truth that Jesus has more power than any force of nature or any human ruler. He is the Lord of lords!

CHAPTER FOURTEEN

You Can Be Salt in a Decaying World

Jesus told His disciples that they were to be "salt" in the world. This may sound like a rather average thing to be, but salt was anything but in Jesus' day. It was exceedingly valuable. The Greeks called salt "divine." The Romans held it in equally high regard. In fact, Roman soldiers sometimes received their salary in quantities of salt—the root for the word *salary* is *salt money*. The Romans also gave us the phrase "He's not worthy of his salt." The Romans had another common saying that nothing was more useful than salt and sun.

On a number of occasions during their captivity in Babylon, Daniel and his three friends—Hananiah, Mishael, and Azariah—functioned as salt, or as a fla-

You are the salt of the earth.
But if the salt loses its saltiness,
how can it be made salty again?
It is no longer good for
anything, except to be thrown
out and trampled by men.
(MATTHEW 5:13)

vorful preservative of the truth about Almighty God in a land badly in need of the truth. They acted as lone voices, speaking to various Babylonian rulers about the sovereignty of God. They upheld the truth that God alone is worthy of all praise, exaltation, and glory. They were ever-present reminders that it is Jehovah God who governs all of the affairs of men, including the affairs of emperors.

Because Daniel went to Nebuchadnezzar to both reveal and interpret the king's dream, Daniel's life was spared but not his alone. The lives of his three close disciples were spared, as well as those of countless wise men, none of whom apparently paid any attention to Jehovah God.

Because Shadrach, Meshach, and Abednego refused to bow to the idol Nebuchadnezzar raised on the plains of Dura, all of Babylon, not just their Jewish brethren, was given the privilege to acknowledge and praise Jehovah God.

In both cases, godly people doing the right thing paved the way for godliness to have an expression in the greater society. That's being salt!

Salt As a Symbol

Salt was used for a number of things in the Jewish world. It was a symbol for the binding of a contract. It was added to grain offerings as a sign of reconciliation (Lev. 2:13). It was given as a present to newborn babies to indicate that the babies were children to whom the covenants of God had been extended.

Certainly our role as Christians today is to bring people into reconciliation with God the Father and to present to the lost the opportunity to come under the covenant of salvation made possible by Jesus Christ.

Salt for Food

Salt was also known to stimulate the appetite and to give flavor to tasteless food (Job 6:6). Years ago a pastor explained to his rural congregation that they were to be a "salt lick for God" in their county—just as a salt lick was placed in a pasture to stimulate cattle to be thirsty for water, so this pastor admonished his congregation to be people who would stimulate lost souls to seek God.

Christians do give "flavor" to this world. Very often the world criticizes Christians as being all alike—bland and no fun. The truth, however, is that the world is prone to fads and filled with pressure to conform to them. Christians have the distinct opportunity to live free of the world's fads and to express themselves with the greatest degree of creativity.

When the apostle Paul sought to compare godly and ungodly lifestyles, he pointed out a number of things he called "the works of the flesh" (Gal. 5:19 NKJV). He noted that the acts of a sinful nature are obvious: "sexual immorality, impurity and debauchery; idolatry and witchcraft; hatred, discord, jealousy, fits of rage, selfish ambition, dissensions, factions and envy; drunkenness, orgies, and the like" (Gal. 5:19–21). Paul gave a stern warning that those who lived like that would not inherit the kingdom of God.

But then the apostle Paul turned to the godly life and he didn't depict this life in terms of a set number of behaviors, but rather character traits. He said, "The fruit of the Spirit is love, joy, peace, patience, kindness, goodness, faithfulness, gentleness and self-control. Against such things there is no law" (Gal. 5:22–23).

In other words, Paul was stating that people who function fully under the guidance of the Holy Spirit and are depicting the character of Jesus in their lives can do thousands upon thousands of different deeds, all of which God approves. There's no law against them! It is the sinners who are trapped in their sin, replaying the same old sins over and over again because they cannot escape their habits.

The Christian is the person enabled to live a truly original life—one that reflects his uniqueness as a person and the many gifts and opportunities God has given to him. Those who follow the crowd into sinful behaviors not only do harm to themselves, but to their peers, their families, their neighborhoods, their schools, their companies, and ultimately, their nation.

Salt As a Preservative

Perhaps the foremost way in which people of the Bible used salt was as a preservative. Foods packed in salt were protected from decay in the hot, arid desert climate of the Middle East. Even fish, one of the most perishable of foods, would not rot if it was packed in salt.

As Christians, we are called to preserve the truth found in God's Word.

Traditions come and go.

Styles of music, and certain styles of preaching, come and go.

The truth of God's Word remains. In fact, Jesus noted that only two things last for all eternity: the Word of God and those who believe it.

How Do We Act As a Preservative?

It's one thing to know that you are called to preserve the truth, it's another thing to know how to do it.

Let's begin by taking a look at how it is that salt loses its saltiness. Salt will cease to be salty if either diluted or polluted. If a half-teaspoon of salt is put in a small glass of water, the water will taste salty. But if a half-teaspoon of salt is put in a ten-gallon container of water, the water will not taste salty. The salt has no effect because it has become diluted. It has lost its saltiness.

If salt becomes mingled with dirt, chemicals, additives, or fillers, it also will lose its saltiness. It will have become polluted.

A Christian loses his witness to the covenant of Jesus Christ, his flavor in the world, and his ability to preserve the truth if he becomes personally polluted by sin. Sinful experiences taint us with their consequences.

Let's be very clear on this point. God forgives us any eternal consequences for our sin the moment we turn to Him to ask for forgiveness and receive the forgiveness He freely and generously offers. He often does not reverse the earthly consequences associated with our sin, however.

A number of years ago a young man murdered his grandparents. He had fallen under the influence of a satanic cult—not because he had been kidnapped and forced into the cult but because he had sought out the cult for identification, intrigued that it offered forbidden activities and strange rituals. He had willfully associated himself with the cult as an act of rebellion against authority in his life. He may have been crazed by the cult at the time he murdered the loving grandparents who had provided a home for him, but he knew right from wrong at the time. A jury convicted him of first-degree murder and sentenced him to die.

This young man heard the gospel while he was in prison and he accepted Christ. He became a Christian and for several years, he wrote letters warning other teens not to follow his example. He witnessed to his fellow inmates about the love of God. He had great peace that God had forgiven him from his sins and that he had an eternal home in heaven.

In spite of his conversion to Christ, this young man was put to death according to the law of the land. He was saved for all eternity, but he was not spared the consequences for what he had done.

This is true in many cases. The consequences of sin often linger for an entire lifetime. For example, people who become addicted to various substances or who participate in various activities are often never fully set free from all temptation to partake of those substances or activities—they must guard their hearts and minds carefully every day. They must trust God week in and week out to help them withstand temptation.

Our lives become polluted by sin, and if we fail to turn to God to ask Him to free us from the entrapment of sin, our witness for Christ Jesus is ineffective.

And how is it that we become "diluted"? One of the ways is by entering into arguments that go nowhere. We fill our minds with what the world says. We construct arguments in our minds against the so-called logic and rationale of those who seek to revise or undermine the Word of God. We engage in endless conversations that never reach a decision point. In the end, if we are not careful, we can spend so much of our time speaking and acting against what is wrong that we fail to pursue what is right!

The world pours its message over us, and over us, and over us until we spend 98 percent of our time and energy dealing with the world's message, and only a minuscule fraction of our time and energy reading, studying, hearing, and telling the truth of God's Word.

It isn't only the world that seeks to overwhelm us with its message. Some in the religious world also seek to do this. There are two great phrases that those who are revisionists—you may call them "liberal Christians," "postmodern church leaders," or Universalists—often use to try to convince people that their opinion is more accurate than the written word of God. The phrases are: "You need to be more open-minded" and "We need to continue a dialogue about this." Be on the alert for those phrases!

The truth is, Universalists and Biblical Revisionists don't want to hear the truth of God's Word because it doesn't allow them to do what they've already decided they want to do. They don't want to hear the truth because they don't like the truth. They will do just about anything possible to justify to themselves and to you that their opinion is just as valid as the Word of God, even though they just came up with that opinion a few minutes ago, a few months ago, or perhaps a couple of decades ago. They will claim to have a "new insight" into God's Word, as if the almighty and eternal God has not been able to communicate clearly for the past several thousand years.

Between 1981 and 1992, I served as a minister in a mainline denomination. I experienced continuous rejection for my orthodox views and ultimately, I was pushed out. The reason? I took a stand and would not compromise my convictions to accommodate the leadership of the denomination.

I discovered that the Universalists and Biblical Revisionists will want to tie you up in endless hours of debate, conversation, dialogue, seminars and symposiums, and discussions if you will allow them to do so. The moment that you definitively state the truth and walk away, they will call you

- bigoted
- closed-minded
- a fundamentalist
- an unloving or hateful person
- a right-winger
- a homophobe
- ignorant
- a Bible thumper.

They do this in part because they cannot fault the truth of what you say and in part because their innermost emotion is hatred for and rebellion against God and everybody associated with Him. Again, they want to pursue the sin they are in because it is pleasurable to them. In some cases, they do not want to be forced to admit that a person who is openly rebellious against God and enters into eternity in that state is lost, usually because a loved one has died without Christ.

These people are living out the prediction of the apostle Paul when he said, "The time will come when men will not put up with sound doctrine. Instead, to suit their own desires, they will gather around them a great number of teachers to say what their itching ears want to hear. They will turn their ears away from the truth and turn aside to myths" (2 Tim. 4:3–4).

Don't allow this endless flow of empty words to overwhelm and dilute you. Neither dilute the potency of what you know to be the truth, or the power of what you speak!

A person once came to me and said, "Pastor Youssef, I hope I did the right thing."

"What did you do?" I asked.

"Well, there's a man who is on a committee with me who always wants to discuss religion. I tell him that I want to discuss relationship with God, not religion. He then moves directly to the topic of some type of sinful behavior and asks me, 'Do you believe that's a sin?' If I say yes, he'll say, 'Aha! Who are you to judge?' I tell him that I love sinners but hate sin, that I believe we are to know the difference between right and wrong and do what is right. Then he says that I am unloving and a bigot."

"It's like talking in a circle," I said.

"Exactly!" he said. "I get a headache just thinking about the hours I've spent talking to this man."

"So what did you do?" I asked again. "You said that you were wondering if you had done the right thing."

"Well," he said, "the last time he started down this track, I said, 'Listen, I'm finished discussing all this with you. I'm a believer in Jesus. You're not. If you believed in Jesus you'd believe what He said in the New Testament. If Jesus hadn't said it, it wouldn't be so convicting for two thousand years! When you get ready to believe in Jesus—then we can talk.'"

"What did he say?" I asked.

"He stared at me in silence. I think he was stunned. He didn't know what to say. Finally, he just walked away."

"How do you feel about what you did?" I asked.

"Great!" the man said. "Like a person who just got free of ropes that had him all bound up."

"Live in that freedom," I said. "Jesus sets people free of endless, unproductive disputes. Go tell somebody about Jesus who needs and wants to hear about Him!"

The apostle Paul gave this advice to Timothy: "Be prepared in season and out of season; correct, rebuke and encourage—with great patience and careful instruction. . . . Keep your head in all situations, endure hardship, do the work of an evangelist, discharge all the duties of your ministry" (2 Tim. 4:2, 5).

Continue to speak up at every opportunity for what you know to be the truth of God's Word.

Walk away from endless arguments that attempt to discount

the truth of God's Word or to discount you as a speaker of the truth.

Don't resort to name-calling or derision. Don't become angry. Continue to act with compassion. Continue to get wise counsel from godly people with mature faith. Continue to live in peace and to speak patiently—but don't give in or back down.

Keep yourself free from sin. Continue to love others by seeking to meet their needs and bless their lives.

In these ways, you will be undiluted and unpolluted salt. It isn't a matter of your trying to be salty or even trying to be salt. You *will* be salt! God will use your life, as well as your words, to convict this world of sin and to preserve what is valuable and eternal.

Establishing Christ's Presence in Your World

Are you harboring a pet sin that dilutes your witness for Christ? In other words, are you doing something that you know is contrary to God's Word, but which you refuse to face? One of the ways you can identify such a sin is by asking yourself: *Would I enjoy discussing this behavior or attitude with a beloved child? Could I explain to the child why this is godly behavior? Would I implore a child to follow this example or pursue this behavior?*

If there is anything in your life that you know is not in keeping with God's Word, repent of it and ask the Lord to help you walk in freedom from it.

Do you frequently find yourself in a debate with others who do not believe God's Word? Is this frustrating to you? Do you feel as if you are being worn down and worn out by the endless debate? If so, find people with whom you can talk about Jesus!

Reflect or Discuss

- What do you believe most pollutes the witness of a Christian?

- What do you believe most pollutes the witness of a church in a community?

Seek to answer these questions by identifying several concrete and practical steps you can take to reverse the pollution process in your own life and in the church.

- What arguments or conversations with nonbelievers do you find most frustrating?
- What might you do to put an end to such arguments or conversations in a way that is loving, and that still leaves the door open for the unbeliever to come to you with honest inquiry about how to receive or serve Christ?

Never compromise in your thoughts, words, or deeds what you know to be the truth of God's Word!

CHAPTER FIFTEEN

You Can Be an Agent of Healing

One way of looking at healing is to look at the end result God desires for healing: wholeness. Jesus repeatedly said to people, "Be made whole."

The biblical understanding of wholeness is that the various aspects of a human being cannot be separated: what damages one part of a person impacts the whole of the person. The Hebrew language has the same root word for both *salvation* and *wholeness*. On a number of occasions Jesus forgave sins as part of a healing process, or He delivered a person from demonic powers as He made him or her whole.

To a great extent we are just now beginning to recognize in the Western world how intricately and inseparably in-

The prayer offered in faith will make the sick person well; the Lord will raise him up. If he has sinned, he will be forgiven. Therefore confess your sins to each other and pray for each other so that you may be healed.

(JAMES 5:15–16)

tertwined are the body, soul (emotions and mind), and eternal spirit of a person. Wholeness should be our goal, and we must not limit our understanding of healing to the mere elimination of a disease or the recovery from an injury.

Especially when we look at the ailments of our society that need healing, we must recognize that there's great need for spiritual repentance and restoration.

What is healing? Too often we confine it to mean the removal of a disease, the breaking of a fever, the knitting of broken bones. Healing, when taken in the context of wholeness, is anything that moves a person in a positive and godly manner toward greater wholeness. Healing always involves change—sometimes the change is small, at other times the change is great. At times the change is rapid, at times it is a slow process.

In the last chapter we talked about salt being a preservative. Salt is also a great agent of healing. Salt heals and cleanses an open wound. The great prophet Elisha once used a bowl of salt to "heal" bad waters, and in turn, heal unproductive lands (2 Kings 2:19–22). Although this seems contrary to the way salt usually functions in a city well or in farming, in this case the salt neutralized poisons in the waters that made them unsuitable for people and for growing plants.

Jesus taught that those who have salt in themselves are in a position to be at peace with each other (Mark 9:50). They are in a covenant relationship with God, cleansed and made useful, and therefore, they are good agents for producing peaceable relationships. Those who are healed, in other words, make the best healers.

As Christians we are to bring people to Christ and thus put them in a position for Christ to reconcile them to the Father. We are to be peacemakers, preaching the gospel of peace, and thus, bring people together within the body of Christ. We are to live in unity with other Christians—not a false, trumped-up unity, but a genuine unity born of a common belief in one Lord, one Savior, one faith (Eph. 4:4–6). We can call people to wholeness, and when we pray for people, we can pray that they be made whole: spirit, mind, body, emotions, relationships, and every other aspect of their beings.

The Flip Side: Disease, Disharmony, Discomfort

The opposite of healing is fragmentation and warlike division. A warring among the cells and tissues of the body produces disease. A warring among people produces disharmony and a lack of peace, including at times lack of unity and peace in the body of Christ. A warring between what a person does and what a person believes produces inner conflict that a person often experiences as frustration, discomfort, or angst.

Any time we encounter something that divides people or separates them from God, we should ask immediately, *Am I the one God desires to use as an agent of healing in this situation?*

How Can We Be Agents of Healing?

What does it mean to be an agent of healing in our world? And more specifically, how can a person who is not one with the world call the world to be whole, at peace, or in unity? By our very definition as Christians, we are a set-apart, holy people, called to be in the world but not of the world. We are "new creatures," no longer walking in the flesh but in the Spirit. How, then, can we make whole something of which we are not a part?

First, we must embrace the fact that we are different from the world. To be just like the world is to have become so diluted or polluted by the world that we are no longer effective. To have an impact on society, we must be distinct from society.

Second, in being different from the world, we are not called to be weird, but rather, to be catalysts. A catalyst is something that causes a change to happen. In the science laboratory, a catalyst is a substance that increases the rate of a chemical reaction without itself undergoing any change. A catalyst is not like the substance it acts upon. It is a change agent only on substances that it is *not* like.

Being a catalyst is certainly the position that Daniel filled in the inner court of Babylon. He was a quiet, resilient, constant change agent. He didn't exert great influence in changing the entire Babylonian bureaucracy; at least we cannot conclude that from what the Bible says. Rather, Daniel exerted great influence on the leader of the Babylonian empire. He was a force for good in the life of the one person who could bring about the most change.

Being a *catalyst for change* is one of the most important ways you can display the power of one.

Throughout history, that is the role many Christians have played. They may not have been the leaders of nations or the founders of great movements, but they have been the close associates or allies of great leaders. They have had the ear of the king and have exerted great influence on the person who could make a major difference in a tribe, region, or nation. Being a powerful force for good can often mean being a catalyst for good in the life of just one person whom God has called you to walk alongside. Don't despise or overlook that role!

Not long ago I heard about a young woman who had volunteered to help with a political campaign for her city's mayor. He was so impressed with her work that he asked her to become part of his permanent staff. As the months passed, he found himself seeking her out to undertake special projects or to give him a young person's opinion about particular issues.

One day he asked her, "Do you think I should mention my faith when I meet with this group?" The young woman said, "Tell me about your faith." She was amazed to hear how deeply committed this man was to the Lord, and therefore, she was surprised he had kept so quiet about his faith for so many years of political life. She said to him, "I am thrilled to hear about how much you love the Lord. The group to whom you will be speaking loves the Lord. I think they'd be delighted to hear about your Christian walk." The mayor took her advice.

This young woman told me later, "That one luncheon event seemed to transform the mayor. He had a new freedom about him—no longer was he hiding his faith. He had a new boldness. He didn't seem to care whether people discovered he was a Christian. That didn't mean he tried to push his religion down other people's throats—he just wasn't the least bit bashful about being a Christian from that day forward."

"Is he still mayor?" I asked.

"No," she said. "He's now lieutenant governor of the state! He became more and more popular after that day he talked about his faith to a church group. He's one of the most popular politicians in the entire state, and the amazing thing is that his opponents, who aren't Christians, can't figure out why. God seems to have his hand on him and he's a great influence for good in getting things done for children and the poor."

Daniel Was a Catalyst God Used

Daniel had a second opportunity one day to be a catalyst for the truth in the life of King Nebuchadnezzar. The Bible tells us God gifted Daniel to interpret dreams and visions. Nebuchadnezzar, it seems, was a man prone to having dreams! This example refers to the second dream Daniel interpreted.

One night King Nebuchadnezzar dreamed about a large tree with beautiful leaves and abundant fruit. Many birds and creatures found shelter in the tree. And then a voice in his dream came down from heaven to say, "Cut down the tree and trim off its branches; strip off its leaves and scatter its fruit." The stump and roots were to be bound with iron and bronze and stay in the field. Then the voice said, "Let him be drenched with the dew of heaven, and let him live with the animals among the plants of the earth. Let his mind be changed from that of a man and let him be given the mind of an animal, till seven times pass by for him" (Dan. 4:14, 15–16).

Nebuchadnezzar was both perplexed and terrified by this dream. He called upon all of his wise men—the top magicians, enchanters, astrologers, and diviners in Babylon—to interpret the dream. They could not. He then called Daniel to interpret the dream.

The Bible gives us Nebuchadnezzar's take on the story: "Daniel came into my presence and I told him the dream" (Dan. 4:8). Our job as Christians is to get in the presence of those who need to hear the truth. God doesn't call us to go in with both barrels of logic and persuasion blazing from our mouths. We simply are to be present, serving in a godly, quiet manner. When people who are troubled or confused see our service and our demeanor, they will initiate conversation with us. It may not happen immediately, but it will happen.

Sometimes they blurt out very deep problems. Sometimes they reveal their needs more timidly. Be patient. Ask for God's wisdom. Look for doors that open for you to speak up. And then, be courageous in walking through those open doors.

We don't know whether the so-called wise men of Babylon could not interpret the king's dream or were afraid to interpret it. We know only that they told the king they could not tell him the meaning. They may have been afraid for their lives if they told him the truth! Many people know what to say, but they are afraid to speak. Don't be counted among them!

Daniel not only could interpret the dream, but he did so. He told the king that he, King Nebuchadnezzar, was the tree. Daniel stated what the king no doubt knew—he had grown great and strong and his "dominion extends to distant parts of the earth." But, Daniel said,

> the Most High has issued [a decree] against my lord the king: You will be driven away from people and will live with the wild animals; you will eat grass like cattle and be drenched with the dew of heaven. Seven times will pass by for you until you acknowledge that the Most High is sovereign over the kingdoms of men and gives them to anyone he wishes. (Daniel 4:22, 25)

Daniel was not like the wise men of Babylon. He was not like King Nebuchadnezzar. He was God's man in that hour—uniquely positioned, prepared, and empowered—and because he was distinctly God's man, he could be a catalyst for change, for healing. He could be a messenger of God's desire to make whole the most powerful man in the world at that time. Daniel boldly said, "Therefore, O king, be pleased to accept my advice: Renounce your sins by doing what is right, and your wickedness by being kind to the oppressed. It may be that then your prosperity will continue" (Dan. 4:27).

What a message this is for us today!

If ever there was a day for the righteous men and women of God to stand tall and say to the world, "Change your ways!" that day is today. Two important things about repentance:

1. We must be bold in our call to repentance. Daniel's message was very clear and very succinct: Renounce your sins. Turn away from doing what is wrong and do what is right. Stop your wickedness.
2. We must be patient in waiting for people to repent. Daniel called King Nebuchadnezzar to repent, but he didn't nag him about it. Nebuchadnezzar, for his part, did not repent. In the short term, it didn't appear that Daniel's interpretation was going to come to pass.

Then, twelve months later, Nebuchadnezzar was walking on the palace roof when he proudly stated, "Is not this the great Babylon I have built as the royal residence, by my mighty power and for the glory of my majesty?" The Bible tells us that those words were "still on his lips" when a voice said from heaven,

This is what is decreed for you, King Nebuchadnezzar: Your royal authority has been taken from you. You will be driven away from people and will live with the wild animals; you will eat grass like cattle. Seven times will pass by for you until you acknowledge that the Most High is sovereign over the kingdoms of men and gives them to anyone he wishes. (Daniel 4:30–32)

God confirmed directly to Nebuchadnezzar what Daniel had foretold. Look for God to do that when you speak as well.

God fulfilled His words to Nebuchadnezzar. The king remained in the field, eating grass like cattle until "his hair grew like the feathers of an eagle and his nails were like the claws of a bird" (Dan. 4:33). Then one day Nebuchadnezzar looked up toward heaven and God gave him back his sanity. He "praised the Most High"—he glorified God with a great statement of praise, saying:

> His dominion is an eternal dominion;
>   his kingdom endures from generation to generation.
> All the peoples of the earth
>   are regarded as nothing.
> He does as he pleases
>   with the powers of heaven
>   and the peoples of the earth.
> No one can hold back his hand
>   or say to him: "What have you done?"
> (DANIEL 4:34–35)

Nebuchadnezzar came to a core truth of life: God is in absolute control of all things.

This is the greatest message underlying all healing: all change that brings a person one step closer to wholeness. It is when we recognize that God is in absolute control, and that He has absolute laws for governing His universe, that we face our need to repent of our ways and to embrace His ways and His sovereignty.

We do not rule our own lives. God will allow us to err only for so long. He will have mercy and long-suffering patience with a godless society for only so long. He will allow godless people to rule with devastating cruelty for only so long. The sooner we acknowledge that truth and repent of the ways in which we are not lining up our lives in accordance with God's truth, the sooner we can be healed and brought closer to God and the wholeness He desires for us.

Jesus said, "It is not the healthy who need a doctor, but the sick" (Matt. 9:12). Jesus was referring to our knowing that we are sick, to our recognizing that we need a Physician, to our being aware that we are in need of God. Before we can ever turn things to right in our own lives, in our families, in our communities, and in our nation, we must first recognize that we are in need of salt being poured into our wounds.

The salt may sting.

But the salt cleanses and allows healing to begin.

The words of truth may sting—in our own hearts, we may feel the prick of conviction from the Holy Spirit. The truthful words we speak in love to others may sting. But the sting of truth can call a person to make the changes that will keep the person—and all the person "governs"—from the devastating consequences of rebellion, disobedience, and sin.

At the same time Nebuchadnezzar's sanity was restored, God restored his honor. He returned to his throne and became even greater than before. The king proclaimed, "I, Nebuchadnezzar, praise and exalt and glorify the King of heaven, because everything he does is right and all his ways are just. And those who walk in pride he is able to humble" (Dan. 4:37).

Do you want to be salt in your world? Seek to be a catalyst for God's healing power.

Establishing Christ's Presence in Your World

What change do you most desire to see in your immediate world or in your community? Who is the key influencer, decision maker, or power player who can bring that change about? In what ways can you begin to serve that person in a quiet, godly way—putting yourself in his presence so he might call upon you? Map out a plan. Make a strategy!

Reflect or Discuss

- In what areas do you desire greater wholeness? What changes do you need to make in your personal life in order to be made whole?
- How important is it for us to seize every opportunity to bring healing to our society—first to ourselves, then to our families, and then to our communities? In what ways do you believe you are equipped, or not equipped, to be an agent of healing? How might you become better equipped?

Seek to be made whole, even as you call others to wholeness.

CHAPTER SIXTEEN

You Can Trust God to Give You the Words to Say

What keeps a person from speaking up to an authority figure who is failing to do what is right or good?

What keeps a person who is attending a school board or city council meeting from going to the microphone to speak in favor of a godly measure or to denounce a decision that may introduce or extend ungodly influence?

What keeps a person from writing to his or her elected representatives in the United States House of Representatives or Senate, or to the president of the United States, about a particular piece of legislation that is coming up for a vote or is about to be signed into law?

One of the top two answers I hear as a response to these questions is this: "I

[Jesus said,] When you are brought before synagogues, rulers and authorities, do not worry about how you will defend yourselves or what you will say, for the Holy Spirit will teach you at that time what you should say.

(LUKE 12:11–12)

don't know what to say." What the person really means is generally, "I haven't figured out what I should say." Most people do not feel comfortable speaking extemporaneously, especially in front of people who have perceived power or fame. They think they should write out, memorize, or at least have made some notes about what they should say if called upon. They don't think they should write a letter because they haven't done enough research on the matter. Even so, they know something important is about to be decided and they have a gut-level opinion about whether it is good or bad!

Jesus told His followers that times would come when they would be questioned by leaders of the synagogue, or by Jewish or Roman authorities. In those moments, Jesus said, "Don't worry. Rely upon the Holy Spirit to teach you what you should say."

Jesus also said to His followers about the Holy Spirit, "When he, the Spirit of truth, comes, he will guide you into all truth." Very specifically, Jesus said the Spirit, whom He also called the Counselor, would "convict the world of guilt in regard to sin and righteousness and judgment" (John 16:13, 8).

Speaking Up for What Is Right

If you have an opportunity to speak, the Holy Spirit will nearly always prompt you to say something along one of these three lines:

I. CALL A PERSON OR GROUP OF PEOPLE TO FOCUS ON WHAT IS MORALLY RIGHT AND WRONG

This includes pointing out that a decision that does not uphold what is right is ultimately a decision that promotes what is wrong. A particular issue may not be cut-and-dried, black or white, but very often there are factors that underlie a decision that can be aligned with the Word of God and judged to be right or wrong.

"But," a person may say, "you can't legislate morality. Here in the United States of America we don't legislate what another person should see as right and wrong."

True. But we also must recognize very clearly that every person who is making laws, or legislating, is a person who has a basic understanding of right and wrong. You may not agree with that person's definitions of right or wrong, but you can challenge him to evaluate a decision according to his own moral understanding. If a person tells you that he is doing what he thinks is right, and you believe that what he is doing is wrong, you can and should ask him to explain why he believes his decision or opinion is right. Keep challenging the person on the why question until you get to the root belief that is giving rise to his decision.

Very often people in leadership positions seem to make decisions on what they think other people want. If you challenge them to expose and explain their personal beliefs, you are putting the moral dimension of a decision front and center. It's time we returned to discussions about what is ethical for our children and the future of our world—which may not be at all what a particular segment of society wants or demands for itself in the present moment.

Be prepared always to know what you believe to be right and wrong. Have reasons for why you evaluate certain decisions as right and others as wrong. If you don't know what you believe about a particular issue, especially the moral and ethical aspects of it, spend some time in the Word of God getting God's opinion on the subject. Talk about moral issues with mature believers in Christ Jesus. Come to some personal conclusions.

Ultimately morality relates to character issues. What are the character qualities in human beings that you desire to see promoted and upheld? If something compels or furthers the character qualities you desire to see in yourself, others, and your children, that is likely something that is right. If, however, something compels or pushes a person to adopt character qualities that you do not want to see in yourself, others, or your children, consider it something that is wrong.

2. CALL PEOPLE TO ACKNOWLEDGE WHAT THEY TRULY BELIEVE

They should speak not only about a particular issue but very specifically as to what they believe about the human beings involved in a particular situation or issue under discussion. People need to be challenged to take a look at what they believe about the value of human life, as well as about the ideal relationship people should have with one another and with God.

There's a spiritual dimension to every decision, law, and judgment. That dimension is directly related to human factors. Decisions aren't just a matter of convenience, efficiency, innovation, budgets, or the common good. Decisions impact human lives, individually and collectively. Every decision impacts how people are either helped or hindered in their walk with the Lord.

3. CALL PEOPLE TO CONSIDER THE LONG-TERM CONSEQUENCES

If a decision is carried to its ultimate long-range conclusion, that decision is likely to bear fruit that is either good or bad. A small decision today can bear huge consequences ten, twenty, or thirty years from now. We need to challenge people in leadership to look at the long view of their decisions, not merely the impact of their decision on this year's budget or next year's election.

Sometimes a person needs to be painted an alternative picture to show what could happen, or what is likely to happen as the result of a particular decision.

If you are called upon for an opinion, or if you are given a public forum opportunity in which to speak, ask the Holy Spirit what He desires for you to say in that moment to that particular audience or group of leaders about morality, beliefs, and consequences.

Bold Words in the Moment

Here is another reason people give me for not speaking up when they have an opportunity to voice an opinion: "I'm nobody. Who cares what I have to say?"

The good news in a democratic society is that you are somebody. You do have a voice. Somebody does care what you have to say. The

Somebody who cares most to hear what you have to say on behalf of the truth is the Lord!

Ask the Holy Spirit to give you a greater understanding of your value to your heavenly Father. Ask the Holy Spirit to give you the courage to act and respond as an emissary of the Most High God. The apostle Paul wrote, "He has committed to us the message of reconciliation. We are therefore Christ's ambassadors, as though God were making his appeal through us" (2 Cor. 5:19–20).

Ours is a message of reconciliation: Get right with God! Be reconciled to God through Christ Jesus. Be reconciled to one another according to God's Word. Live in agreement with God's commandments. Live in peace with one another as you both seek to live in agreement with God.

Never lose sight of the fact that you are an ambassador of heaven, your true home, to this earth—your temporary dwelling. God has a purpose for you as His representative in your world, to express His will, His commandments, and His love to the people you encounter.

Very often the person who feels deeply moved to speak up for the truth in the heat of the moment is a person who speaks from a greater depth of personal passion and belief. The Holy Spirit seems to speak through the person in a more powerful way. Don't decry your lack of opportunity to prepare. Trust God to guide your thoughts and your words as you speak.

A man said many years ago, "I was trying to decide what God wanted me to do with my life and my father-in-law said, 'Son, it's easier to steer a car once the key has been put into the ignition switch and the car is moving.'" So, too, with our words. Very often the Holy Spirit waits for us to open our mouths and begin to speak before He imparts to us exactly what we should say!

Understanding the Writing on the Wall

Finally, ask the Holy Spirit to reveal to you any hidden agenda, any deceit, any underhanded maneuvering, or any illegal or immoral aspects of a decision or law that is being debated or discussed. Ask Him to bring to light the hidden lie.

That is precisely what happened on a particular night when Daniel was summoned to see Belshazzar, the son of Nebuchadnezzar. While Belshazzar was hosting a great banquet for a thousand of his nobles, he ordered that the gold and silver goblets that his father had taken from the temple in Jerusalem be brought out so that his guests might use them. As Belshazzar and his noblemen, along with their wives and concubines, were drinking wine from these goblets, they were praising the gods of gold, silver, bronze, iron, wood, and stone. Suddenly the fingers of a human hand appeared and wrote a message on the plaster wall of the banquet hall. "The king watched the hand as it wrote. His face turned pale and he was so frightened that his knees knocked together and his legs gave way" (Dan. 5:5–6).

Belshazzar immediately summoned the wise men—the enchanters, astrologers, and diviners—to interpret the message. He promised that whoever could read the writing would be clothed in purple, given a gold chain to wear, and be proclaimed the third highest ruler in all the kingdom.

Even with that incentive, the king's wise men could not read the writing. At that, the king "became even more terrified and his face grew more pale. His nobles were baffled." The queen, overhearing the commotion in the banquet hall, entered the room and said to the king, "Don't be afraid. I know somebody who can help you." She told the king about Daniel, who in the time of Nebuchadnezzar "was found to have insight and intelligence and wisdom like that of the gods." The queen pointed out that Daniel "was found to have a keen mind and knowledge and understanding, and also the ability to interpret dreams, explain riddles and solve difficult problems" (Dan. 5:9, 11–12). The king took her advice and called Daniel to tell him what the writing meant.

Daniel didn't have time to prepare a speech. He didn't even know what the meeting was about! But Daniel had something no other man had that night: integrity, character, and the Word of God hidden deep in his heart.

When he heard the offer of gifts and high rank, Daniel said to the king, "You may keep your gifts for yourself and give your rewards to someone else. Nevertheless, I will read the writing for the king and tell him what it means" (Dan. 5:17).

What wisdom there is in that opening statement from Daniel! He made it clear that he was not seeking personal profit. It is very important as you seek to influence others for good that you go to the person with that kind of integrity—no hidden agenda of your own and no desire for personal fame or gain.

Daniel reminded Belshazzar that his father, Nebuchadnezzar, had been a very powerful man, but when he became a prideful ruler, God had deposed him and stripped him of his glory. He reminded Belshazzar how Nebuchadnezzar had eaten grass like cattle in the field until he had acknowledged the Most High God as sovereign over the kingdoms of the earth.

Daniel then said, "But you his son, O Belshazzar, have not humbled yourself, though you knew all this. Instead, you have set yourself up against the Lord of heaven. . . . You did not honor the God who holds in his hand your life and all your ways" (Dan. 5:22–23).

Finally, Daniel interpreted the four words that had appeared on the plastered wall: "*Mene, Mene, Tekel, Parsin.*" These words meant: "God has numbered the days of your reign and brought it to an end. . . . You have been weighed on the scales and found wanting. . . . Your kingdom is divided and given to the Medes and Persians" (Dan. 5:26–28).

Daniel didn't mince words. He spoke the truth. He called Belshazzar to recognize the fundamental error of his ways: his arrogance before God in doing what was wrong even though he knew what was right. To use temple vessels for wine toasts to pagan gods was about as wrong as wrong could be!

Belshazzar, for his part, was so proud there wasn't even a hint of repentance in his response. He insisted that Daniel be clothed in purple, given a gold chain, and named the third highest ruler in the kingdom.

That night, however, Belshazzar, king of the Babylonians, was slain. Darius the Mede took over the kingdom.

Do you know what to say?

Say what is the truth of God's Word.

Say what is necessary for producing good character in others and moral behavior in society.

Say what honors God.

Say what uplifts the value of the person—what upholds integrity, dignity, and quality of life, including a good spiritual quality of life.

Say what is right not only for today, but for the future.

And if you have to point out what is wrong—and where wrong will lead—do so. Don't be afraid to be one lone voice speaking the truth.

God will cause your words to resonate in the hearts of those who need to hear it. Even if they refuse to heed your words of wisdom or warning, God will honor you for speaking what He has prompted you and "taught" you to speak.

Establishing Christ's Presence in Your World

Do your homework. Find out what is on the upcoming agenda—perhaps the next meeting of the city council or school board, or perhaps the bills your state legislature or the United States Congress is considering during the next session. Choose one issue, ruling, or impending law. What does your heart tell you about the importance of this decision? Is it morally good or bad—will it lead to better character and more ethical behavior? Is it rooted in God-fearing beliefs? Is it a good decision for the future? Express your opinion—put down your thoughts in writing or show up at the meeting. Make a difference!

Reflect or Discuss

- Many times we see in retrospect whether a decision was good or bad—we have the advantage of seeing what has happened as a moral consequence. If the following three issues were coming to a decision today, what would you say with regard to them? Take into consideration moral issues of right and wrong, character-building issues, and long-term consequences.

1. Taking all prayer out of the schools
2. Keeping the Ten Commandments from being posted in schools
3. Legalizing abortion

- How might your opinions and reasoning about these issues relate to issues such as the following? Again, focus on moral issues and long-term consequences:

1. Stem-cell research on fetal tissue
2. Legalizing same-sex marriages
3. Removing the phrase "under God" from the Pledge of Allegiance

Trust God to tell you what to say. Rely on Him to give you the courage to open your mouth and begin to speak. And then *speak up*!

CHAPTER SEVENTEEN

You Can Be a Beacon in a Storm of Evil

One of my favorite stories through the years is of a ship's captain who was navigating his large vessel through a violent storm. He spotted a light off in the distance, straight ahead, and he had his communications expert send a signal: "Change course to avoid a collision with us." He indicated the exact direction and degree of change he wanted the other vessel to make.

The signal came back, "Change course. Go fifty degrees to the north."

The captain was enraged. He immediately ordered his subordinate to send a second message, "Change course!" This time, in addition to dictating the specific degrees and direction he wanted the other ship to take, he added

[Jesus said,] You are the light of the world. A city on a hill cannot be hidden. Neither do people light a lamp and put it under a bowl. Instead they put it on its stand, and it gives light to everyone in the house. In the same way, let your light shine before men, that they may see your good deeds and praise your Father in heaven.
(MATTHEW 5:14–16)

to his command the size of his own ship and the importance of its cargo.

The signal came back, "Change course! Go fifty degrees to the north . . . immediately."

The captain was beside himself as the distant light drew closer and closer in the rain-driven winds that were lashing against his ship. Determined not to yield, he signaled a third time, "Change your course!" This time he added to his command information about his own rank as a naval officer.

The reply came back, "Change course! I'm the keeper of the lighthouse."

Called to Be Light

Jesus said to His followers that they were the "light of the world." Light is visible—it is direct, external, seen. Light serves two great functions:

1. LIGHT GUIDES

If you have ever been out on a mountain trail on a moonless night, you know the value of having a strong flashlight! Light can keep you and other hikers with you on the right path. In the same way, the light of our example can help others around us stay on the right path in their walk with the Lord. We can help people find their way through a difficult circumstance by continuing to point them toward Jesus and the hope He offers to them.

Those who display the power of one function as guides to other people.

2. LIGHT WARNS

Just as the lighthouse sends out a signal warning to a ship that it is about to crash on the rocks, we are to warn people when we see that they are about to enter a danger zone.

Those who display the power of one serve as warning signals.

This is not to say that everybody we warn will either want to hear our warning or respond kindly to it. Jesus said, "Light has come into the world, but men loved darkness instead of light because their deeds were evil" (John 3:19). Some people want the lights to stay off so they can continue their wicked ways unchallenged and at times, uninformed.

The story is told of a nomad in the deserts of the Middle East. He awoke one night extremely hungry. He knew he was carrying a large cargo of dates so he opened one of the bags and bit into a date. It was delicious! He decided he'd light a candle and have himself a little feast. He lit the candle and bit into a date, and found a worm inside it. He tossed it aside and bit into another date, only to find a worm inside it as well! He continued to bite into date after date, only to find a worm in each one. Finally he blew out the candle and ate all the dates he wanted!

That's the way some people are. They don't want to know right from wrong. They don't want to have to think about consequences and character issues. They simply want to meander through life doing what they want to do, pursuing whatever whim or passion comes up next.

The apostle Paul challenged the Ephesians,

You were once darkness, but now you are light in the Lord. Live as children of light (for the fruit of the light consists in all goodness, righteousness and truth) and find out what pleases the Lord. Have nothing to do with the fruitless deeds of darkness, but rather expose them. For it is shameful even to mention what the disobedient do in secret. But everything exposed by the light becomes visible. . . . This is why it is said:

"Wake up, O sleeper,
rise from the dead,
and Christ will shine on you."

(EPHESIANS 5:8–14)

A Light in Dark Babylon

Daniel and the three friends he influenced most directly—Hananiah, Mishael, and Azariah—were like stars in the velvet black of night. They were like candles of light in the midst of dark Babylon. Let me point out to you three valuable principles about being a light for the Lord, each of which these brave young men embodied.

First, we are called to reveal the Lord, not ourselves. We aren't called to put the light on our own accomplishments or behavior. We are called to put all of the focus on Jesus! We are to be like the moon that reflects the sun and has no light of its own—we are to reflect the *Son* of God before the world.

Nothing you can do, win, or earn is capable of getting you a passport to heaven. Your entrance to heaven will be solely on the basis of your believing in what *Jesus* did, won, and accomplished on the cross for your benefit. Our lives as Christians are not about us. Our lives are all about Jesus Christ.

Second, we are *not* called to shine a light into other people's eyes, which serves only to blind them.

Often Christians are so exuberant in their proclamation of the truth that they beat up other people emotionally and mentally in trying to speak truth into their lives. They become irritants, not helpers. We are always called to shine the light of Christ with compassion to those who are walking in darkness. Jesus saw people as sheep without a shepherd and He was moved with compassion to guide them gently into places where they could be protected and nourished. A shepherd in Bible times didn't use dogs or whips to prod sheep forward. A shepherd used only his voice to lead sheep to follow him. In like manner, we must approach other people with compassion and generosity. It is our love that will compel them to follow us all the way to Jesus, and then to begin to follow Him as their Great Shepherd.

Third, light doesn't make noise. It is calm and steady in its silence. Certainly there are times when we need to make noise—and should—as we stand up for the truth. During the vast majority of our time, however, we are to be about our work in the attitude God spoke through the prophet Isaiah: "In repentance and rest is your salvation, / in quietness and trust is your strength" (Isa. 30:15).

What are others to see in us as we light the way to Jesus? Good deeds. Jesus said, "Let your light shine before men, that they may see your good deeds and praise your Father in heaven" (Matt. 5:16).

People really don't care what we know, until they know we care.

People "hear" our deeds far more than they hear our words.

People respond to what we do for them, not what we seek to have them do for us.

Your greatest influence on other people is going to come as you *serve* them, with godly character and a generous, compassionate spirit.

Show me a person who is looking for a helper. . . .

Show me a person who is looking for a good spouse. . . .

Show me a person who is looking for a loyal employee. . . .

And I'll show you a person who wants someone who has impeccable integrity and character, and who is willing to work hard with a loving and compassionate attitude. The person who embodies those traits is going to be heard, rewarded, sought out, and honored. Furthermore, the person who embodies those traits is going to be someone who has great influence for Christ, even in the most ungodly environment.

Daniel, as far as we know from the Scriptures, did not seek to be in the continual presence of the kings he served—Nebuchadnezzar, Belshazzar, or Darius. His routine was not a daily advisory session to the king. Rather, his daily routine was to do the work of governing that the king had given to him. On occasion, when these kings were perplexed and frightened, these kings sought out Daniel.

Hananiah, Mishael, and Azariah never sought to stand out in a crowd. They simply remained standing when everybody else bowed to an idol.

Faithful, godly service in doing what was right before God over a period of years was the hallmark of Daniel and the three who were directly influenced by him. The infrequent days when they had great impact on the Babylonian empire were days God engineered for His purposes in the lives of His people, as well as the Babylonians.

The same is true for us.

Not every day is going to be a day when we change the world.

But . . . every day is a day when we need to be ready to speak up for the truth or to honor the Lord. Every day is a day when we need to be doing our work with the utmost integrity and the noblest character traits. Every day is a day when we need to be obeying the commandments of God and seeking the face of God so that we might be in a deeper and deeper relationship with Him.

We are to walk every day believing that today just may be the day of days for which God created us and placed us on this earth. And even if our day is not the most exciting, stellar day of influence we can imagine, it is the day the Lord has made for us to walk out a godly example to others. We are to live in a way that is always attractive to the Lord, and that always attracts other people to want to know Him.

People Will Seek You Out

You can count on two things:

1. PEOPLE GRAVITATE TO CONFIDENT WISDOM

People will seek you out when they are confused. People want clarity and good answers. They want to know what they don't know. They want insight and direction. They will turn to you because they see you as a godly and obedient person with high principles and a moral compass. They will turn to you because they recognize you as a person who walks with assurance, knowing without doubt that you are headed for heaven and Jesus is by your side. They will want your advice, even if they feel this only subconsciously or intuitively.

People without direction naturally gravitate to people who have direction. People who feel no inner confidence naturally gravitate to people who have that confidence.

When people come to you in their confusion, that will be your opportunity to speak the Word of God to them!

2. PEOPLE GRAVITATE TO COMFORT

People will seek you out when they are worried and don't feel at all prepared for the future. A pastor friend once said to me, "The two best times I've found to talk to people about their spiritual futures are when they are about to undergo surgery or when they are about to die." Those are times of great fear for most people.

In the last twenty years, what was the one Sunday when, as a whole, the churches in America were most full? The Sunday after the September 11th terrorist attacks on the World Trade Center of New York City and the Pentagon in Washington, D.C.! People were frightened. They wanted answers that gave them hope — they wanted a firm foundation of faith on which they could stand.

When a person with great fear or anxiety comes to you, he is seeking you out because you seem to have the quiet confidence of faith and assurance that only Jesus can impart to the human heart. That is your opportunity to speak words of faith and comfort!

Don't put your light under a bushel — don't try to hide who you are in Christ. For your life to be effective, and fulfilling, you must live out your faith in good deeds, to which you add your faith-filled, truth-filled words.

Establishing Christ's Presence in Your World

List three things that you believe cause people to worry the most these days.

List three things that you believe cause the most fear in people.

What is your response or answer from God's Word to these fears and anxieties? Identify specific Bible verses that address worry and fear. Memorize them!

Then . . .

Identify a person you know who seems particularly anxious. Make a lunch date with that person or invite that person to go with you and your family to a special event. Find an opportunity to speak words of encouragement and comfort to that person—words that are based upon God's Word and loaded with truth, compassion, and a desire to point the person toward Christ.

Reflect or Discuss

- Reflect upon an experience in which someone came to you asking for advice or comfort. How did you respond? What were the results? Do you wish you would have responded differently? How so? What can you do to prepare yourself for such an opportunity in the future?

Walk in the light of Christ and others will want to walk with you.

CHAPTER EIGHTEEN

You Can Live a Consistent Life—
All Your Life

Of all the stories in the Bible, the story of Daniel in the lions' den is one of the most famous and most popular. Perhaps that's because so many of us have felt at times that we were about to be tossed into a lions' den, at least figuratively—or perhaps we feel that we are in one right now, hoping with all of our ability that God will keep the mouths of the lions tightly shut!

Just as you received Christ Jesus as Lord, continue to live in him, rooted and built up in him, strengthened in the faith as you were taught, and overflowing with thankfulness.
(COLOSSIANS 2:6–7)

Few people seem to know, however, that this experience in Daniel's life came when he was an old man, probably in his eighties. No person is ever too old to display the power of one!

By the time of this incident, Daniel had been in Babylon more than sixty years. The king in the story was the third

emperor that Daniel had served, and he knew little of Daniel's early years, although he had perhaps heard that Daniel had a way of understanding dreams and visions.

Darius was not a name—it was a title that literally meant "Maintainer." The Medes and the Persians had worked together to overthrow Belshazzar, the son of Nebuchadnezzar, and Darius, who was in his sixties, was put in the position of leadership until the power balance between the Medes and Persians could be sorted out.

Darius set up a different style of administration over the Babylonian empire—120 satraps or governors under the administration of three men, one of whom was Daniel. Very quickly it became apparent to Darius that Daniel was superior to all of the governors and the other two administrators. Darius planned to put Daniel in charge of the whole kingdom. That, of course, didn't sit well with various Medes and Persians who, no doubt, thought they should have a bigger piece of the spoils of victory.

In a political power play, the administrators and governors who were about to be demoted, at least in their own eyes, tried to find grounds to make charges against Daniel for the way he conducted government affairs. They couldn't find anything to pin on Daniel. They could find no corruption or negligence in him—he was absolutely trustworthy and diligent. One of the greatest powers one can exercise is that of trustworthiness.

What a track record! Most people who serve in public office for sixty years have made some mistakes or errors in judgment that their opponents can uncover and use against them! Daniel had a clean record. So, the administrators said, "We will never find any basis for charges against this man Daniel unless it has something to do with the law of his God" (Dan. 6:5).

Sounds like today's headlines, doesn't it? If nothing can be found in the work record of a godly politician, his opponents nearly always seem to go after his Christian testimony, trying to label him or her "right wing," "conservative," or "fundamentalist"—as if these were evil things to be!

Daniel's enemies begin to look closely at Daniel's religious practices and discovered that three times a day—morning, noon, and night—Daniel got down on his knees facing Jerusalem, his childhood home and the location of the temple, and he did two things: Daniel gave thanks to God and he asked God for help.

Daniel's behavior should have been a clue to his opponents! Show me a person who is praising God diligently and faithfully three times a day for sixty years and I'll show you a person who is powerful in his faith and in his relationship with the Lord!

Show me a person who asks God for help three times a day and I'll show you a person whom God very likely leads hour by hour into making the right decisions and choices that lead to success! Daniel's superlative record was no doubt directly the result of his personal discipline of praise and prayer—but rather than adopt such a discipline for themselves and succeed as Daniel had, Daniel's political enemies sought to undermine Daniel by using his religion against him.

The plot Daniel's enemies concocted was clever. They talked King Darius into issuing a decree that anyone who prayed to any god or man during the next thirty days rather than to Darius should be thrown into a den of lions. The word *pray* literally means to "make a request"—it means to look to someone for an answer or help.

Darius, of course, desired to be the absolute leader of the empire so he perceived such a decree as something of a loyalty oath. The administrators' request sounded reasonable on the surface—nobody should have been making petitions or giving political loyalty to anybody but Darius. He quickly agreed and allowed the royal decree to be published and the ruling put into effect for thirty days.

Darius was a Mede and the law of the Medes and Persians was such that any decree the leader of the people made could not be repealed.

Daniel's Faithful Response

When Daniel learned that this decree had been published, he "went home to his upstairs room where the windows opened toward Jerusalem. Three times a day he got down on his knees and prayed, giving thanks to his God, just as he had done before" (Dan. 6:10). In other words, Daniel didn't change anything he had been doing for sixty years. He maintained his steadfastness of faith!

Daniel could have said, *Oh, it's only for thirty days. I'll just take a break from praise and prayer and resume my daily devotional discipline next month.*

Daniel could have said, *I'll just shut the window. Nobody will know what I'm doing. I'll pray downstairs in a closet. God will see and hear me there and I won't get in any trouble.*

Daniel didn't make any compromise. He continued to do what he had always done. He was consistent in doing the right thing.

That's the key point for you to understand in this part of the story: Daniel consistently did what honored God. He consistently offered praise. He consistently prayed for help. Daniel was consistent in his very open witness that he believed in and trusted the God of Israel.

Consistency is vital in displaying the power of one. Daniel was a powerful threat to his opponents not only because of his position as a high-ranking official in Babylon, but because of his reputation for consistency, integrity, and godly wisdom.

It's important not to overlook that Daniel's open window faced Jerusalem. No doubt he had requested that very room. Daniel prayed in the morning, at noon, and in the evening—the times of the sacrifices in the temple. His prayer life was in sharp contrast to that of the Chaldeans, the so-called wise men of Babylon. The Chaldeans were night people. They convinced the superstitious emperors of Babylon that the gods had given the Chaldeans power to govern whether the sun came up each morning. They exercised this power by keeping fires burning all night. Once the sun came up, which they took credit for, they slept until late afternoon. They were, in a very real and concrete sense, associated with the rulers of darkness.

Daniel prayed during the daytime! He worshiped the God who governed the affairs of all men. He worshiped the God who said,

"Let there be light" and then used the light to create all the known universe. Daniel was a person of the Light. He walked in the light of God's law and trusted God to help him be a light to God's people and to those under his leadership. What a contrast between Daniel and the other wise men.

While they slept, he worked!

While they slept, he prayed!

While they slept, he produced a sixty-year track record of excellence!

And while they danced around fires to ensure that the sun would come up the next morning, Daniel slept in peace knowing that Jehovah God, not the Chaldeans, was in charge of all things. Don't ever forget that all of this is the good harvest resulting from exercising the power of one.

Daniel had a deep assurance in him after six decades of faithfully trusting God. The apostle Paul wrote to the Romans, "If we live, we live to the Lord; and if we die, we die to the Lord. So whether we live or die, we belong to the Lord" (Rom. 14:8). Daniel knew this truth deep in his soul.

Do you?

Have you settled once and for all the question *How big is God?*

Is God bigger than your enemy?

Is God bigger than the decree of an ungodly person?

Is God bigger than the forces conspiring against you?

Is God bigger than any emperor who may control your behavior but has no control over your faith or your spiritual destiny?

The Marks of a Consistent Life

Daniel demonstrated three great hallmarks of the consistent Christian life in his response to this decree by Darius.

First, to be consistent is to do the right things *daily*. Jesus called His followers to live in the day, to be mindful of the moment. He said in teaching them to pray that they were to petition their heavenly Father in this way: "Give us this day our daily bread." "Daily bread" didn't refer only to physical food. It referred to everything that gives life meaning and fulfillment.

Take a hard, long, and honest look at your own Day-Timer or daily schedule. It will tell you if you are consistent in your spiritual life. What you do every day, day in and day out—regardless of weekends, vacations, or time off—tells a great deal about who you are. Your daily habits produce your character, and your character dictates your destiny.

Second, to be consistent is to offer praise and seek God's help *often*. Praise and prayer aren't Sunday chores. They are to be part of our lives every waking hour. The apostle Paul wrote to the Thessalonians: "Pray continually; give thanks in all circumstances" (1 Thess. 5:17–18). This means that you always direct your mind toward thinking and saying, "I praise You, God, for who You are in my life at all times. I thank You, Lord, for all You have provided, are providing, and have promised to provide."

To pray continually means to continually be on the alert as to what God desires for you to say or do, continually seeking to understand what He wants to accomplish and how He wants you to participate in His work. Continual prayer and thanksgiving are the way we set our hearts, minds, and souls toward the things of God.

How often do you think or say, "Thank You, Lord" or "Praise God"?

How often do you ask the Lord to help you during the average day?

The frequency with which you turn to God to praise Him, thank Him, or seek His help is a strong indicator about the consistency of your faith.

Third, to be consistent is to look to God *first* in all things. This does not just mean to look to God first thing in the morning, although that is a very good time to offer praise and to seek God's help. It means to put God *first* any time you need to make a decision. It means that when you see something good or beneficial, your *first* thought is to praise God as the Creator, Provider, and

Protector—the Giver of every good and perfect gift! (James 1:17).

The consistency of your daily praise, prayer, and trust in God is what creates your reputation. These hallmarks are at the very core of your being a power-of-one person!

When Daniel heard Darius's decree, he knew he needed to get his mind on *God*—not on the decree, not on his political enemies, not on the lions in the den, not on Darius. He needed to know what *God* wanted him to do. He needed to remind himself that *God* was and would always be the Supreme Ruler sitting on the throne of his heart.

What is your first response when trouble arises, or when an enemy takes a jab at you, or when you realize that you are being trapped in an evil plot? Your first response is an indicator of the consistency of your faith.

Daniel's consistency in serving God was the key to his lifetime of success.

Spiritual consistency is what allows a person to live a lifetime free of corruption.

Spiritual daily disciplines are what set up a person to live a lifetime of diligence, without negligence.

Spiritual trustworthiness in the things of God creates a foundation of trustworthiness that others can rely upon.

Daniel's faith was the key to his success, his reputation, and his inner strength. The same is true for you. Your faith is what will sustain you when the decrees don't go your way and opponents conspire against you.

Establishing Christ's Presence in Your World

Look at your daily schedule over the last three months. What do you do consistently every day?

Think back over your last two days. How often did you turn to God to praise Him, thank Him, or ask for His help?

Think back to the last problem you faced—or perhaps think

about the problem you are currently facing. Did you talk it over with God as your first response?

Reflect or Discuss

- How difficult is it to maintain a daily devotional discipline? What are the challenges you face or have faced in developing a daily habit of praise and prayer?
- What keeps a person from openly praising or praying— that is, where others might see or overhear? How important is it to be open in your witness to Christ? To what extent are we to refrain from making our prayer lives an exhibition before other people? What is God's balance between being open in our witness and yet not calling attention to our own piety?

Consistency is tested daily.

CHAPTER NINETEEN

You Can Know Peace
in Perilous Times

Daniel was set up.

Have you ever had other people conspire against you to undermine your influence or your integrity?

Have you ever had people band against you after you have taken a stand for the truth or have called for the right thing to be done? Have they rejected or ridiculed you in hopes of discouraging you into giving up your position or your fight for justice?

Have you ever had someone denounce you for your faith or for the spiritual disciplines of your life?

Daniel's enemies had set him up not only for a fall, but for a death sentence.

King Darius had issued his decree that anyone who prayed to any god or person

[Jesus said,] Peace I leave with you; my peace I give you. I do not give to you as the world gives. Do not let your hearts be troubled and do not be afraid.
(JOHN 14:27)

other than Darius for thirty days would be thrown into the lions' den. The decree was published. And the ink wasn't even dry on that published decree when Daniel's political enemies went to the king and spoke against Daniel, saying, "Daniel, who is one of the exiles from Judah, pays no attention to you, O king, or to the decree you put in writing. He still prays three times a day" (Dan. 6:13).

Darius was greatly distressed at this news. He realized immediately that he had been tricked into taking action against his most trustworthy and skilled administrator. The Bible tells us that Darius made every effort until sundown to save Daniel from the decree's punishment, which was to be carried out that night. The men opposing Daniel went as a group, however, to remind Darius that he could not overturn or change the decree, and so the king gave the order to have Daniel thrown into the pit. As Daniel was thrown into the lions' den, the king said to him, "May your God, whom you serve continually, rescue you!" (Dan. 6:16).

The Lion and the Lions

What was the purpose of a lions' den? The lion was a major symbol of power in Babylon. Only the emperor was allowed to keep lions, and he did so in pits close to the palace. The caged lions ate the meat scraps from the king's table, and their very existence served as a deterrent against an emperor's political enemies. To be fed to the lions was a punishment reserved primarily for traitors and political foes—in other words, it was the supreme penalty for anybody who had the stupidity or audacity to challenge the power of the emperor. In essence, if you went up against the power of the lion figuratively and lost, you became the victim of the lion literally.

Don't miss the subtlety of what's happening here! Daniel was a Jew. He was from Jerusalem. The city of Jerusalem—the capital city of Judea—was technically in the territory given to the very small tribe of Benjamin, but it had been ruled for centuries by leaders from the very large neighboring tribe of Judah. Judea was comprised of just these two tribes. The symbol for the tribe of Judah is the lion! Jesus is called the "Lion of the tribe of Judah" (Rev. 5:5).

This showdown between the rulers of Babylon and Daniel is a spiritual battle. Daniel didn't pick the fight against the gods of Babylon; rather, the worshipers of the gods of Babylon unwisely picked a fight against the God of Daniel!

This was a battle between the lion of Babylon and the Lion of God!

The Underlying Spiritual Battle

Any time you take a stand against ungodly behavior, you are going to be subject to spiritual attack by those who do not worship Jesus as Savior and Lord or acknowledge that Jehovah God is God Almighty! The enemies that may come against you and seek to overthrow you, undermine you, or otherwise attack you may appear to have a political, social, or even organizational agenda. If they are coming against you on the basis of your faith, however, the devil is using them to attack you. The end goal is to discourage you, destroy your reputation, cause your downfall, and to kill any influence you might have for the gospel.

Don't be naïve.

Understand who your real enemy is.

Understand what your real enemy is up to.

Understand what's at stake.

Understand the power of your own integrity and faith.

And also have a clear understanding that when you stand up for God and do what is right in His eyes, God stands up for you!

The devil never stops trying to tempt or attack Christians. The Bible tells us that he is relentlessly in pursuit of us. In fact, the Bible tells us that the devil "prowls around like a roaring lion looking for someone to devour!" (1 Pet. 5:8). The picture is the same one painted in Daniel: the devil as a roaring lion comes to take on the Lion of the tribe of Judah who is resident by the power of the Holy Spirit inside you! It's lion vs. Lion all over again.

When Daniel was thrown into the pit of lions, a stone was placed over the top of the den and sealed with the signet ring of Darius and the rings of the nobles. The king returned to his palace and spent the night not eating, sleeping, or being entertained. He was a troubled man! He knew that he had been tricked and had done wrong. Those who feel guilty are always highly anxious.

The Bible doesn't say so, but Daniel appears to have had a good night's sleep. The ungodly king was awake because of the lions; Daniel wasn't affected.

What a contrast! It's one we see again and again in our world. Ungodly people are filled with anxiety in trying to manipulate others, turn things to their own advantage, or win points to secure favor. They toss and turn all night, wondering what more they might do to bolster their position. Godly people take a stand for what is right or speak up for the truth and sleep soundly, knowing they have done the right thing.

The next morning, at the first light of dawn, Darius hurried to the lions' den and called to Daniel in an anguished voice, "Daniel, servant of the living God, has your God, whom you serve continually, been able to rescue you from the lions?" (Dan. 6:20).

Daniel answered, "O king, live forever! My God sent his angel, and he shut the mouths of the lions. They have not hurt me, because I was found innocent in his sight. Nor have I ever done any wrong before you, O king" (Dan. 6:21–22).

The king was overjoyed and ordered that Daniel be lifted immediately from the den. He had fulfilled the decree by throwing Daniel in the den, but there was nothing that said after throwing him in, he couldn't pull him out after one night!

No wound was found on Daniel. The Bible adds, "Because he had trusted in his God" (Dan. 6:23).

God's Delivering Power

Let me point out to you three great truths about the way God works.

First, God delivers His people *in* the lions' den, not just *from* the lions' den. So often we ask God to keep us from being thrown into a controversy or difficult position, and we believe God is somehow greater if He spares us from trouble. The truth is, Jesus told us that we will face tribulation in this life, and that tribulation will come, in part, because of our witness for Him. If you are actively living a Christian life, you are going to be actively persecuted for it, by someone, at some time, in some way. God's promise to us is that He is with us always, and He delivers us in the time of trouble.

Second, God rewards those who go through persecution trusting in Him. If we die from the persecution, He rewards us in eternity—that's His promise. If we endure until the persecution has run its course, He rewards us as well. Jesus said,

> Blessed are those who are persecuted because of righteousness,
>   for theirs is the kingdom of heaven.

> Blessed are you when people insult you, persecute you and falsely say all kinds of evil against you because of me. Rejoice and be glad, because great is your reward in heaven, for in the same way they persecuted the prophets who were before you. (Matthew 5:10–12)

If you retain your trust in Christ when you are persecuted, God *will* reward you in ways that are exceedingly greater than anything you can imagine.

The Bible tells us, "Daniel prospered under the reign of Darius and the reign of Cyrus the Persian" (Dan. 6:28).

Third, God has a way of dealing with our enemies that is far more powerful, and often more demanding, than anything we could engineer.

Very often we end the story of Daniel prematurely. The Bible goes on to say that the political enemies who had sought Daniel's demise were rounded up at the king's command. Darius wisely discerned that they were the true enemies of the state. Daniel's political foes, along with their families, were thrown into the lions' den. And just in case you thought that the lions hadn't harmed Daniel because they weren't hungry, read what happened to Daniel's enemies: "Before they reached the floor of the den, the lions overpowered them and crushed all their bones" (Dan. 6:24).

You can't begin to know exactly what awaits those who are doing evil, persecuting you for your faith, devising means of harming you, or participating in decisions that are contrary to the Word of God. God has a plan for them! He is counting on you to do the right thing so He can do His thing.

A Greater Good

That still isn't the end of the story of Daniel and the lions' den. Not only was Daniel's life spared and then blessed; not only were Daniel's enemies destroyed; but there was a greater good involving people who probably didn't even know what had happened behind the palace walls.

> Darius wrote to all the peoples, nations and men of every
> language throughout the land:
>
> ". . . I issue a decree that in every part of my kingdom people
>   must fear and reverence the God of Daniel.
> For he is the living God
>   and he endures forever;
> his kingdom will not be destroyed,
>   his dominion will never end.
> He rescues and he saves;
>   he performs signs and wonders
>   in the heavens and on the earth.
> He has rescued Daniel
>   from the power of the lions."
>
> (DANIEL 6:25–27)

Daniel's praise in the upper window of his room turned into a great outpouring of praise to God across the empire! Darius didn't just suggest that the people consider praising God. Darius issued a decree that people must fear and revere the God of Daniel.

The more a people praises God—whether that people is a family, a school, a church, a community, a nation—the more God reveals Himself to that group of people. As people praise God for who He is—the omnipotent, omniscient, and loving King of the universe—the more those people understand that God alone rescues and saves, performs signs and wonders, and oversees a kingdom that doesn't end. The more a group of people understands what God does, the more those people are likely to turn to God to seek His help and His forgiveness.

Never underestimate the power of your praise and prayer to bring deliverance to your own life or the lives of your family members.

Never underestimate the power of praise and prayer in your church to bring about a mighty revival of souls saved and lives changed. Never underestimate the power of praise and prayer in a church to impact an entire community, city, state, or nation for Christ.

Never underestimate the power of praise and prayer across a nation to bring about a wave of respect, reverence, and worship of God.

Establishing Christ's Presence in Your World

If you don't have a daily habit of praise and prayer in your life, start now.

Join with another person to praise God together and pray together for needs that you recognize as being mutually important to your church, school, community, or the nation. Make a commitment to continual praise and prayer.

Reflect or Discuss

- Why do we fear persecution?
- Why do we fear opinions of man over the opinion of God?
- In what ways has faith overcome fear in your life?

Never forget: when God takes on an enemy, God always wins.

CHAPTER TWENTY

You Can Stand Against Immorality

Throughout the Bible, from cover to cover, we have example after example that God is who God says He is. God is capable of doing what God says He is capable of doing. God's principles are sure and lasting—they do not change according to the whim of fashion or the opinions of man. God is infinite and sovereign. His commandments are lasting and absolute. And the good news is that God blesses those who use the power of one.

The opponents of Daniel who were destroyed in the den of lions were just one example of God's justice being exacted according to God's laws, not the laws of the Medes and the Persians or any other man-made law. God is perfectly ca-

You shall not commit adultery.
(EXODUS 20:14)

pable of defending Himself—He doesn't call upon us to speak up for what is right because He needs our defense. He calls upon us to stand for righteousness and to proclaim the truth of His Word because He wants us to have the privilege of participating in His divine purposes and plans. He wants us to have a role in winning the world to Christ Jesus and He wants to reward us for living according to His commandments. God's desire is to bless us in this life and live with us forever in the splendor and perfection of heaven.

It is our responsibility to live in accordance with God's plan, not God's responsibility to live up to our expectations, to fall in line with our way of seeing things, or to do everything we desire Him to do so we can gratify our own lusts and passions.

Daniel's Own Dream—and Its Interpretation

Daniel, the great interpreter of dreams, had a dream. It did not frighten him, but it did trouble him in his spirit and disturb his mind. It was a dream about four beasts—a lion, a bear, a leopard-like creature with four heads and wings like a bird, and a fourth beast that had ten horns and was capable of destroying the other beasts. This fourth beast was eventually slain and its body destroyed in a blazing fire.

Then Daniel saw

> one like a son of man, coming with the clouds of heaven. He approached the Ancient of Days and was led into his presence. He was given authority, glory and sovereign power; all peoples, nations and men of every language worshiped him. His dominion is an everlasting dominion that will not pass away, and his kingdom is one that will never be destroyed. (Daniel 7:13–14)

Daniel asked an angel to tell him the meaning of his dream, and the angel revealed to him that the four great beasts were four kingdoms that would develop on the earth. "But," the angel said to

Daniel, "the saints of the Most High will receive the kingdom and will possess it forever—yes, for ever and ever" (Dan. 7:18).

The angel went on to tell Daniel: "The sovereignty, power and greatness of the kingdoms under the whole heaven will be handed over to the saints, the people of the Most High. His kingdom will be an everlasting kingdom, and all rulers will worship and obey him" (Dan. 7:27).

That is not only the good news of the Bible, but the greatest news of all time! God wins every battle He fights. And that is what the power of one is all about. Those who put their faith in Christ Jesus not only live forever but live victoriously forever.

Daniel concluded after God revealed to him the meaning of his dream: "This is the end of the matter" (Dan. 7:28). It was a definitive statement as far as Daniel was concerned. The saints will one day rule the kingdoms according to the will of God and the rules of heaven. God's plans will be enacted and His purposes will be accomplished. The way God's kingdom in heaven functions will one day be the norm on this earth.

God's Laws Are for Man's Good

One thing we know about all kingdoms is that they have laws. In the book of Daniel, various kings decreed various things. Their will was done. In the heavenly realm, God, the sovereign King of the universe, has decrees. They are a reflection of His will for how human life should be governed. They are His plan for the morality and ethical behavior of His people. They are rules that are for the good of His people—they reflect the way life works best.

Adultery, for example, doesn't help or bless anybody! It eventually hurts the two people who engage in it. It hurts the innocent spouse or spouses. It hurts the children. It tears apart families and friendships. It creates suspicion and ill will in a circle far bigger than the two people involved.

Murder doesn't help or bless anybody! It results in death and vengeance and long-standing bitterness and pain. It never solves a problem but instead creates thousands upon thousands of problems, big and small.

Covetousness and greed don't help or bless anybody. What a person with a covetous spirit gains is never enough. What a person gains through covetousness breeds estrangement. In the end, a society that is covetous is a society filled with backstabbing, manipulative, lying, cheating people.

A person may think his particular sin has no far-reaching consequences. That person is wrong. This is the opposite of the power of one. This is the downfall of one.

It is no secret that righteousness is under attack. We are the ones today who are being attacked for having morals, rather than those without morals being called into question! We are told we should feel ashamed for being intolerant or unloving, rather than sinners being told they should be ashamed for trying to cram their sin down our throats. We are the ones being told today that we must allow for sexual deviance and immorality, rather than those without morals being told that they must change or face consequences associated with their rebellion against God's laws.

All around us we see people who are determined to rule their lives and to enact rules that govern the behavior of others in a way that is contrary to what God has decreed, and therefore contrary to the will of heaven and to the way the world will one day function under God's saints.

God's Way vs. the World's Way

Perhaps in no way is the difference between God's way and the world's way more obvious than in areas related to sexual behavior and marriage.

God has said, "You shall not commit adultery" — which is sex between two people, at least one of whom is married (Exod. 20:14).

The world says, "It doesn't matter how many spouses you have. Divorce and remarry until you find the person who makes you happiest."

The world says, "No person can be faithful to just one spouse. It isn't natural."

The world says, "Your marriage will be more interesting and exciting if you do a little experimentation on the side."

God has said, "You shall not commit fornication"—which is sex between two unmarried people. Some Bible translations refer to this as "sexual immorality" or "sexual impurity" (see Eph. 5:3; 1 Thess. 4:3).

The world says, "Have sex with whomever you want—just use protection."

The world says, "It is acceptable to have sex with a person if you are both consenting and you love each other."

The world says, "Don't worry about what other people may think. You aren't hurting anybody. You have a right to be happy and to have your needs met."

The world says, "Live together—there's really no reason to bother with marriage vows or ceremonies."

God has said, "Sexual immorality of all kinds is wrong" (see Lev. 18).

The world says, "Different people have different needs and desires. We need to be tolerant."

The world says, "No doubt there's a reason for people to engage in these sexual behaviors. We need to try to understand what drives a person to engage in these behaviors."

The world says, "Don't be too quick to judge others. Everybody isn't alike."

God has said, "I am the Lord your God. Obey what I say" (see Lev. 18:4).

The world says, "No."

The world is wrong and those who follow the dictates of their own passions and lusts, with no respect for God's law, will be destroyed. The Bible is very clear on that point. The person who chooses to ignore or rebel against God's commands—and then passes laws that are contrary to God's commandments or who encourages others in any way to ignore or rebel against God's commands—is in grave danger.

Reestablishing Sexual Morality

The messages that directly or indirectly portray sexual immorality are rampant in our culture. If you don't think so, you haven't turned on your television set recently. If you question the pervasiveness of sex as a tool to sell everything from toothpaste to automobiles, watch a couple of hours of prime-time television and stay in your chair when the commercials come on.

If you question whether young people know far more than their grandparents ever dreamed of knowing about perverse sexual behavior, watch an hour of MTV (music television) or rent an R-rated movie that is supposedly off-limits to teenagers under the age of seventeen but which is usually marketed directly to teenagers!

If you question whether all of these sexual messages are having an impact on marriages in our nation, take a look at divorce and marriage statistics provided by any reputable survey group.

Don't think the church is immune to this. In some parts of the nation, the divorce rate among Christians is just as high as or higher than the divorce rate among non-Christians. Research has repeatedly shown that just as great a percentage of teens in the church as teens in the world are watching R-rated movies.

So What's a Person to Do?

First and foremost, if you are unmarried, you need to make a personal commitment to sexual abstinence until marriage. If you are married, you need to make a personal commitment to sexual fidelity in marriage.

Second, you need to make an equal commitment to sexual purity. Don't just make a commitment about your behavior. Make a commitment about what you will see, hear, and take into your thought life. Make a commitment about what you refuse to fantasize about. Make a commitment that you will govern your thoughts and attitudes and stay pure in your mind and heart.

Jesus said,

You have heard that it was said, "Do not commit adultery." But I tell you that anyone who looks at a woman lustfully has already committed adultery with her in his heart. If your right eye causes you to sin, gouge it out and throw it away. It is better for you to lose one part of your body than for your whole body to be thrown into hell. And if your right hand causes you to sin, cut it off and throw it away. It is better for you to lose one part of your body than for your whole body to go into hell. (Matthew 5:27–30)

Jesus wasn't talking about physical mutilation here. He was talking about denying yourself the privilege of looking at and handling things that should not be looked at or touched! Why? Because what you think about becomes what you will eventually do. The more a person fantasizes about immoral sexual behavior, the more the person begins to make a subconscious plan for acting out that behavior. The more a person begins to put himself into a position to be enticed by immorality, the more that person is going to be tempted until the day he gives in to temptation.

This is not a new pattern. It's been the pattern of sexual impurity and sexual infidelity since the beginning of time! There's nothing new about the so-called New Morality. It's just the Old Morality repackaged!

Don't think you are strong enough to withstand the pressures of a continual diet of sexual messages.

Don't think you are above temptation. Even the strongest Christian can be tempted to do evil.

Don't think you are immune to enticement.

Guard your thoughts. Take captive every stray imagination and idea that is contrary to what God has commanded.

Third, refuse to tell or listen to sexual jokes and stories. Walk away from them. If people criticize you for being a prude, a Goody Two-Shoes, or a naïve, out-of-sync person, so be it. Choose to be a person who stands for decency, and who is respectful of people of the opposite sex. Choose to be a person who believes sex is a gift from God that must be used correctly in order to be enjoyed fully.

Don't listen to tales of sexual exploits, or to a friend telling you sexual desires or fantasies.

Fourth, if you are a parent, get smart about what your children or teenagers already know. Have open and honest discussions with your children about why they need to abstain from sexual intercourse until they are married and why they should remain sexually pure. If you don't know the reasons why, become informed yourself before you talk with your children or teens. Sexual immorality isn't a matter only of disease or unwanted pregnancies—the emotional impact is deep and lasting.

Taking a Stand against Society's Moral Leniency

It isn't enough that you take a personal stand for morality in your own behavior and thoughts, or in the behaviors of your immediate family or circle of friends. There's also good reason for you to take a public stand for morality!

How might this be done?

Refuse to see movies or buy DVDs that are sexually explicit or that portray immoral behavior. If enough people exert their personal purchasing power, Hollywood will eventually get the message.

Don't buy novels that promote immoral sexual fantasies. If enough people exert their personal purchasing power in this arena, publishers will also get the message.

Insist that sexually immoral books be kept out of school libraries.

Insist that sexually immoral Web sites be off-limits on school computers and your own home computers.

Voice your opinion to those who manufacture products and use advertising methods that are sexually explicit or enticing.

Voice your opinion to your legislators—both in the United States House of Representatives and the Senate on any bill that in any way denigrates marriage between one man and one woman, that allows for pornography or portrayals of sexual abuse, or that opens the door to the destruction of innocence in children.

If someone in your family—perhaps even your spouse—is facing great sexual temptation or has fallen into sexual sin, begin to pray in earnest for that person, and don't stop praying.

Above all, don't be passive about this. The power of one is not limited to being exercised in the public arena. The home is often where the power of one can be clearly practiced.

Anything that chips away at a person's identity in Christ is harmful. An unending stream of sexually immoral messages does just that. And what happens on the individual level also happens on a societal level. Those things that chip away at the morality of a society eventually break the ability of that society to be a force for good in the world.

Establishing Christ's Presence in Your World

Make a decision about how you not only can but will seek to establish greater sexual purity in your life—and then follow through on that decision.

Identify at least one way in which you can make a positive stand for sexual morality in your workplace or community—and then take that stand.

Reflect or Discuss

- In what ways do we need to guard ourselves from becoming tempted by sexual messages even as we seek to become more informed about what is being fed to society at large, especially to our children and teens?
- In what ways are issues related to sexual immorality related to abortion rates, divorce rates, depression and suicide rates, anxiety rates, and the consumption of mind-numbing substances?
- To what extent does sexual immorality impact a person's basic understanding and value of self? To what extent

does sexual immorality impact a person's relationship with God?

Never forget: what you see and touch becomes what you think about, and that, in turn, becomes what you do.

CHAPTER TWENTY-ONE

You Can Stand Against Amorality

When people break God's moral code or absolutes, even a blind person can see that something is broken. The world has almost as much definition for morality as the church. The world knows, for example, that adultery is wrong. Those in the world will say it's wrong. But the world also shrugs and says, "It's wrong, but it happens, and that's just the way it is. Live and let live." This reduces immorality to a norm. When that happens, we are dealing with *amorality.*

Amorality is the stance that there is no such thing as a moral standard for everybody—there are no absolutes that apply to all people. Rather, the amoral person concludes that every person can decide his or her own moral standards.

My brothers, if one of you should wander from the truth and someone should bring him back, remember this: Whoever turns a sinner from the error of his way will save him from death and cover over a multitude of sins.
(JAMES 5:19–20)

Jesus warned against amorality. He said as part of the great Sermon on the Mount,

> Do not think that I have come to abolish the Law or the Prophets; I have not come to abolish them but to fulfill them. I tell you the truth, until heaven and earth disappear, not the smallest letter, not the least stroke of a pen, will by any means disappear from the Law until everything is accomplished. Anyone who breaks one of the least of these commandments and teaches others to do the same will be called least in the kingdom of heaven. (Matthew 5:17–19)

By "the Law," Jesus was referring to the Ten Commandments and the laws of God as He gave them to Moses. These commandments were not the creation of Moses; rather, they were the divine word of God given to Moses. Jesus went on to say, "But whoever practices and teaches these commands will be called great in the kingdom of heaven" (Matt. 5:19).

God's laws matter.

They are to be obeyed.

There's a reward for obeying them, and a serious consequence for disobeying them.

We need to be very serious in our understanding of the commandments of God. The Bible makes it clear that to be accepted by God we must keep the Law of God perfectly, all the time. I can hear some saying, "Who can do that?" The answer is no one, other than Jesus Christ. He is the only man who was able to keep the commandments perfectly. And no one can ever be saved just because he is doing his level best to keep the commandments.

This is where the uniqueness of the Christian faith shines through. The Bible tells us that when we admit our sins, God forgives our sins (1 John 1:9). Not only that, but Jesus promised that those who received God's forgiveness would be given the indwelling presence of the Holy Spirit, and that the Spirit would help them desire a godly life and obey God's commandments.

The Keys to Full Obedience

We must guard against two things in regard to obedience.

I. NO EDITING ALLOWED

First, we must avoid the tendency to pick and choose which laws we like and therefore are willing to obey. The Word of God is not subject to our editing.

In fact, the power of one can be manifested best when there is an integration between what we claim to believe and how we practice that belief.

Years ago the great baseball player Babe Ruth argued with an umpire. He said, "Forty thousand people know that was a ball!" The umpire calmly replied, "Mine is the only opinion that counts."

The same is true for God's Word. God's "opinion" about what is right and wrong is the only one that counts. We must know what God has said in His Word, believe it to be true, and then live out the truth of His commandments to the best of our ability every day of our lives.

That's what Jesus did, and that's what He calls us to do. Three times in a very short period of time, Jesus said to His followers, "If you love Me, you will keep My commandments" (see John 14:15, 21, 23).

What were the commandments of Jesus? They were the same commandments of the Old Testament, taught by the only man who ever completely fulfilled those commandments in His own life. Jesus summed up the commandments of God by saying, " 'Love the Lord your God with all your heart and with all your soul and with all your mind.' This is the first and greatest commandment. And the second is like it: 'Love your neighbor as yourself.' All the Law and the Prophets hang on these two commandments" (Matt. 22:37–40).

Jesus not only told His disciples what to do, He showed them how to love the Lord God with total commitment—heart, soul, and strength. He did this by living out the commandments. Scripture declares that He was a man with no sin, no deceit, no guile (1 Pet. 2:22). Jesus showed His disciples how to love their neighbors by healing them, delivering them from evil, loving them with generosity, teaching them about the goodness and greatness of God, and in the end, dying for their sins so they might have the opportunity to experience God's forgiveness and receive the gift of eternal life (John 3:16).

2. NO DISCOUNTS APPLY

Real error always begins when we begin to discount whether God has really said something. That was Eve's first fatal error! The devil came to her in a beautiful disguise to ask her, "Did God really say you can't eat that fruit?" He planted seeds of doubt in Eve's mind and she watered them! You can say that Eve used the power of one negatively by persuading Adam to follow her in disobedience.

That's the same trick the devil uses today in countless groups across our nation. He says about the absolutes of God's Word, "Did God really say that?" If a person reads the Scriptures and concludes that yes, it appears God really did give an absolute command, the devil has a follow-up question: "But did God really mean that?" If a person concludes, "Yes, God probably did mean that," the devil has yet another follow-up question: "But did God really mean that for this generation, this century, this environment, this age? Or was that just a rule for Bible times or for a people less civilized or less sophisticated?" The devil's final question is one that has tripped up even mature Christians: "But did God really mean that command for you? Aren't you beyond that command? Hasn't He called you to a new freedom in Christ that removes you from having to keep that command? Hasn't He blessed your ministry or called you to a special level of leadership so that you don't have to keep all these rules that are for the common mass of sinners?"

No wonder Jesus said the devil "is a liar and the father of all lies"! (John 8:44).

Not long ago I heard about a leader of a mainline denomination who quoted the Scripture: "Do not lie with a man as one lies with a woman; that is detestable" (Lev. 18:22), then said God wasn't really referring to homosexuality. In fact, he wasn't sure that text was translated accurately, since it wasn't until the nineteenth century that *homosexuality* had a definition.

These were arguments that I was subject to day in and day out in my mainline denomination. My response often was, "Who are you kidding? God Almighty doesn't know the human heart? God doesn't know what is right and wrong for the creatures He created—spirit, mind, and body? God doesn't understand how the human mind works and how it seeks to experiment with and move beyond the boundaries of decency?"

This man, not unlike thousands upon thousands of people in our society today, discounted the Word of God as being invalid, inappropriate, inapplicable, and irrelevant. As Ted Koppel once said, "The Ten Commandments are not the Ten Suggestions." God has put limits on human behavior, and when we strain and rebel against those limits, we not only do ourselves harm, but we harm the greater society.

The Law of God reveals our sinfulness and inadequacy so that we might own up to our need of God's forgiveness and accept the sacrifice Jesus made on the cross on our behalf.

Jesus reveals that it is possible to obey God and to live a godly life in the flesh. He is our role model for all morality.

The Holy Spirit enables us to keep the laws of God, and our reliance upon Him must be daily.

The power of one helped Daniel to stand in a world with changing emperors and a thousand or more gods. It didn't really matter to the Babylonians which gods a person chose to serve—what mattered only was that the people appeased the gods so that the sun would continue to rise, crops would continue to produce, women would continue to bear children, and calamities would be kept to a minimum.

Daniel stood in a world that couldn't care less about moral standards or spiritual absolutes, and he said repeatedly, "I serve the one and only living God." Daniel knew and no doubt recited innumerable times the words that every good Jew knew:

> Hear, O Israel: The LORD our God, the LORD is one. Love the LORD your God with all your heart and with all your soul and with all your strength. These commandments that I give you today are to be upon your hearts. Impress them on your children. Talk about them when you sit at home and when you walk along the road, when you lie down and when you get up. Tie them as symbols on your hands and bind them on your foreheads. Write them on the door-frames of your houses and on your gates. (Deuteronomy 6:4–9)

Hear the commandments of God. Let them sink into your spirit. Choose to express your love for the Lord by obeying Him.

Impress the commandments on your heart and on the hearts of your children. Sink them deep into your mind so that they become your mind-set.

Talk about the commandments. Reinforce them in your heart.

Keep the commandments at the forefront of your thinking and doing. Evaluate all the behavior in your home and in your workplace, community, and church according to the commandments.

This is the way to keep from becoming amoral in an amoral world!

What Keeps Us from Taking a Stand?

Many Christians would agree with me that we must know and obey the commands of God, and that we must believe that God has established absolutes of right and wrong with regard to human behavior. These Christians, however, remain strangely silent when it comes to public statements about morality. By "public statements," I'm not referring to writing a letter to the editor, giving a speech, or standing up on a soapbox on the corner of a busy intersection outside City Hall. Making a public statement about morality can be speaking up in a conversation over lunch or in insisting that guests in your home abide by your family rules regarding morality.

Why do we fail to speak up and exert the power of one? There are at least four main reasons.

1. FEAR OF REJECTION

Many times people fail to speak up on moral issues because they want other people to like them more than they fear God's displeasure. Others fear that they will be ostracized, criticized, or harmed in some way for speaking up. Jesus said about this:

> Do not be afraid of those who kill the body but cannot kill the soul. Rather, be afraid of the One who can destroy both soul and body in hell. . . . Whoever acknowledges me before men, I will also acknowledge him before my Father in heaven. But whoever disowns me before men, I will disown him before my Father in heaven. (Matthew 10:28, 32–33)

2. A DESIRE TO MAINTAIN PEACE

Sometimes people don't speak up because they don't want to rock the boat. They don't want to confront because they don't want to create an uncomfortable situation. Jesus very clearly said, "Do not suppose that I have come to bring peace to the earth. I did not come to bring peace, but a sword" (Matt. 10:34). Jesus wasn't talking about war. He was saying that godly people, by their very example, are going against the grain of society. They are going to create friction and make waves if they truly are living out the commands of Jesus to love God and love others as themselves. They are going to cause people to be uncomfortable because their attitudes, words, and behaviors are going to bring feelings of guilt and shame to those who are in open rebellion against God.

Let me assure you: nobody was ever won to Christ or was ever convinced to do the right thing because a Christian remained silent about Jesus or about the truth of God's Word!

3. FEAR OF COMING ACROSS AS JUDGMENTAL

When Jesus called us not to judge, He wasn't telling us to turn a blind eye to sin! There's a very distinct contrast between true submission to God Almighty and the practices of false religions, between truth and hypocrisy, between holy standards and self-righteousness, and between genuine faith and false appearances of piety. We need to be able to judge right from wrong and to discern false prophets from true prophets (see Matt. 7:15).

Only God judges motives. We are to judge fruit. Jesus was very bold in judging the fruit He saw in some of the religious leaders of His day:

> Make a tree good and its fruit will be good, or make a tree bad and its fruit will be bad, for a tree is recognized by its fruit. You brood of vipers, how can you who are evil say anything good? For out of the overflow of the heart the mouth speaks. The good man brings good things out of the good stored up in him, and the evil man brings evil things out of the evil stored up in him. (Matthew 12:33–35)

4. LACK OF COMPASSION

Some people simply don't understand fully the consequences associated with amorality. If they did, surely they would feel more compassion for those who are subject to those consequences. Perhaps some people simply don't care enough about the fate of other people to want to pull them from the fires of hell. They don't care enough to cry, "Watch out!" or "Pay attention!" before their friends, neighbors, or coworkers aimlessly wander over the edge of a cliff or fall into a pit of miry clay!

May God give us the sensitivity to care deeply about what is right and wrong.

May God give us the courage to care enough to speak up and tell others the commandments of God and encourage them to obey them.

May God give us the compassion to care about the fates of other people and about our society as a whole.

Establishing Christ's Presence in Your World

Evaluate how much you care about moral standards and values. Do you really care that others around you are amoral? Do you care enough to confront them?

Identify a particular example of amoral behavior in your world. In what ways might you call people to a new awareness or understanding of the commandments of God?

Reflect or Discuss

- How can we as Christians overcome the fear of rejection? How might we overcome the fear of making waves? How might we overcome a fear of being called "judgmental"?
- What instills compassion in a person? How might we become more compassionate toward those who are amoral or immoral?

Let me tell you a story about how God often uses compassionate confrontation. The late Larry Burkett, former host of the popular radio program *How to Manage Your Money*, came to the Lord through a compassionate confrontation.

Larry told me how he debated with the pastor of the church his wife attended in Florida. They went in circles until finally the pastor stormed out of the house. Then he came back in and said, "Larry, you are going to hell."

That statement rattled Larry and shattered all of his intellectual vaunt. A few days later, Larry gave his life to Christ.

Care enough to confront evil. Fear God enough to obey Him.

CHAPTER TWENTY-TWO

You Can Stand on a Sure Foundation of Absolutes

Several years ago it seemed that every time people agreed with something someone said, they responded, "Absolutely!"

I found this a little odd, especially in a society that has so little regard for absolutes. Very few people, it seems, truly want anybody to be absolutely correct or absolutely without fault. If they did, they'd all want Jesus!

Certainly very few people are willing to evaluate their own behavior or are willing to be evaluated by others against a standard of absolutes—most people want others to "cut them some slack," "understand" when they fail, give them a little "leeway," and allow them to "go with the flow" of the latest fad without question or criticism.

I the LORD do not change.

(MALACHI 3:6)

Perhaps at a deeper level, however, our society does crave the security and stability inherent in absolutes. If something is *absolute*, then it is what it is! It doesn't change. It doesn't morph, warp, or flip out. If something is an absolute, we can count on it. When absolute principles are upheld, there's a sense of constancy and the comfort of knowing that the foundation is sure. When absolute consequences follow absolute principles, there's a sure rate of return. There's no waffling, no flying by the seat of your pants, and no wondering when the other shoe will drop.

On the one hand, we want relativity when it comes to our own morality and spirituality.

On the other hand, we want a sure thing when it comes to interest rates, future prognostications, home security systems, the vows our spouses made at our weddings, and the promises of those who agreed to help us or serve on our committee.

On the one hand, we want God's mercy as we go our own ways.

On the other hand, we want God's justice when other people trample us.

On the one hand, we want to do what we want to do.

On the other hand, we want to know that we will wake up tomorrow morning healthy, a little wealthier, and a whole lot happier.

We can't have it both ways.

Either we believe in the absolutes God established and choose to live by them. Or we believe in our own made-up code of life.

We either live according to God's promises that have reliable outcomes, or we live by our own set of principles and morals that provide momentary pleasure but are inevitably flimsy and fluctuating and ultimately lead to heartbreak, failure, and death.

Perhaps the most absolute of truths is that there is an absolute truth!

What Daniel Counted Upon as Absolutes

Living in the amoral, immoral, and ever-changing world of Babylon, Daniel relied on at least three absolutes. They were the foundation for his life. They are also foundation stones for those who want to display a godly power-of-one influence today.

1. GOD DOES NOT CHANGE

Daniel knew that God is *immutable*, which is a good theological word meaning that God is the same yesterday, today, and forever (Heb. 13:8). God's character and nature do not change. Because of that He is utterly trustworthy. What God says He means. What He says He does.

Man, on the other hand, does change. He changes his mind when he perceives that a different opinion is more advantageous to his cause. He changes his feelings when he finds a different feeling more pleasurable and gratifying to his lusts. He changes his commitments when he finds a different commitment to be more lucrative in satisfying his material needs or beneficial in meeting his desire for fame, power, or love.

Because Daniel trusted in a God who did not change, Daniel did not change. He was consistently who he was in more than sixty years of administrative leadership and eighty years of life! Even evil peers evaluated him as a man who was trustworthy, without compromise or corruption.

2. GOD'S WORD DOES NOT CHANGE

It is just as wrong today as it was thousands of years ago to lie, steal, kill, commit adultery, or covet your neighbor's possessions. It is just as right today as it was thousands of years ago to love the Lord your God with a singleness of heart, to put your total trust in God, to honor the name of the Lord, to keep the Sabbath, and to honor your parents.

Jesus said, "Heaven and earth will pass away, but my words will never pass away" (Matt. 24:35).

"But," you may say, "there are some parts of the Bible that just don't apply to my life."

That simply isn't true. The apostle Paul wrote to Timothy, "All Scripture is God-breathed and is useful for teaching, rebuking, correcting and training in righteousness, so that the man of God may be thoroughly equipped for every good work" (2 Tim. 3:16–17).

There's something to be gained from every verse in the Bible. You will learn something about the nature of God, the nature of human beings, or about the relationship God desires to have with man or that God desires to see human beings have with one another. You will find passages that cause you to stop what you are doing, change what you are doing, or start doing something new. You will find the wisdom of the ages about how to succeed—doing fulfilling work, enjoying good relationships, accomplishing worthy goals, and experiencing the abiding presence of the Lord.

God's Word is for you. It is for now. And it is forever.

Daniel knew that. And because he believed that God's Word does not change, he knew that he could count on God's Word being true regardless of circumstances or the various schemes of Babylon's emperor. He knew that *right* before God would always be *right*, and *wrong* before God would always be *wrong*.

He knew that what God promised would come to pass.

He knew that what God provided would be enough.

He knew that when God acted it would be in time.

He knew that what God authorized would be established and his only power was in obeying.

Do you have a full confidence deep within that God's Word is true for you in the situation you are facing right now?

3. MAN DOES NOT CHANGE, APART FROM GOD WORKING IN THE HUMAN HEART

Daniel no doubt also knew that the human heart didn't change. Belshazzar was just as perplexed and frightened by the sovereign intervention of God in his life as his father, Nebuchadnezzar, had been. We may like to think that we have advanced as human beings through the ages, but that simply is not true. People are just as cruel, abusive, greedy, unscrupulous, and hateful as they have ever been. They are just as bigoted, manipulative, corrupt, and crafty as ever. Nations and tribes are just as territorial and prone to war.

Technology has changed.

Factual knowledge has increased.

Borders and boundaries have changed.

Fashions, fads, structures, borders, and organizations have come and gone.

But the human heart has not changed. There has been no dramatic worldwide improvement in crime rates, rates of drug usage, sales of pornographic material, amounts of benevolent giving, quality of life for the poor, or the percentages of people who die from viral and bacterial infections. As a human race, we are just as sick, selfish, and sinful as we have ever been.

The only genuine and lasting change possible in the human heart is a change that God initiates and completes at man's invitation. God has given to every person a measure of faith and a great degree of free will. Man can exercise these to invite God in or push God away. Man can exercise his faith to believe for great and mighty miracles or rebel in free will and attempt to run as far from God as possible. Unless God changes a person's desires, hopes, and character—at the person's invitation—the nature of a person does not change.

If, however, a person willingly invites the Lord to do a work in his heart, that person can experience a total inner makeover! His mind can be renewed and his attitudes adjusted to the degree that he begins to think as God thinks, respond as God responds, and feel as God feels. His life can undergo a complete transformation so that he no longer is the "old man" but is a "new creature" in Christ Jesus! (see 2 Cor. 5:17). He can experience the power of the Holy Spirit at work in his life to the degree that he is capable of putting off sinful habits and characteristics and "put[ting] on the new self, created to be like God in true righteousness and holiness" (Eph. 4:24).

It is only by the power of God at work in a human being's heart that a person can be "renewed in knowledge in the image of its Creator" (Col. 3:10).

The great news of the gospel is that God says He will do this transforming work in us if we ask Him to do it, and as a result, we will become the people with whom God desires to live in eternity. We will become all that we can be in Christ Jesus! God Himself will be the "author and finisher of our faith" (Heb. 12:2 NKJV). He will help us to run our course and "win the prize" for which God has called us heavenward (Phil. 3:14). He will give us renewed minds so that we can know His "good, pleasing, and perfect will" (Rom. 12:2).

Daniel wasn't just a smart, good-looking Jewish boy who grew up automatically to be a wise, successful top-drawer administrator in Babylon. Daniel was wise because he knew the absolutes about God, God's Word, and the human heart, and he trusted in those absolutes. He based his life on them. They molded his thinking, guided his decision making, guarded his choices, and were the foundation for his faith.

Read God's great promise through the ages to all who will hear and heed God's commandments, relying on His absolutes to be their firm foundation:

> If you accept my words
>   and store up my commands within you,
> turning your ear to wisdom
>   and applying your heart to understanding,
> and if you call out for insight
>   and cry aloud for understanding,
> and if you look for it as for silver
>   and search for it as for hidden treasure,
> then you will understand the fear of the LORD
>   and find the knowledge of God.
> For the LORD gives wisdom,
>   and from his mouth come knowledge and understanding.
> He holds victory in store for the upright,
>   he is a shield to those whose walk is blameless,
> for he guards the course of the just
>   and protects the way of his faithful ones.
> Then you will understand what

is right and just and fair—every good path.
For wisdom will enter your heart,
    and knowledge will be pleasant to your soul.
Discretion will protect you,
    and understanding will guard you.

(PROVERBS 2:1–11)

Put It to the Test

The only way you can know with certainty that God never fails and that His Word is always trustworthy is to put God to the test. God invites you to do so! The Bible gives us a powerful statement about this through the prophet Malachi. Read it carefully:

"I the LORD do not change. So you, O descendants of Jacob, are not destroyed. Ever since the time of your forefathers you have turned away from my decrees and have not kept them. Return to me, and I will return to you," says the LORD Almighty.

"But you ask, 'How are we to return?'"

"Will a man rob God? Yet you rob me.

"But you ask, 'How do we rob you?'"

"In tithes and offerings. You are under a curse—the whole nation of you—because you are robbing me. Bring the whole tithe into the storehouse, that there may be food in my house. Test me in this," says the LORD Almighty, "and see if I will not throw open the floodgates of heaven and pour out so much blessing that you will not have room enough for it. I will prevent pests from devouring your crops, and the vines in your fields will not cast their fruit," says the LORD Almighty. "Then all the nations will call you blessed, for yours will be a delightful land," says the LORD Almighty.

"You have said harsh things against me," says the LORD.

"Yet you ask, 'What have we said against you?'"

"You have said, 'It is futile to serve God. What did we gain by carrying out his requirements and going about like mourners before the LORD Almighty? But now we call the arrogant blessed. Certainly the evildoers prosper, and even those who challenge God escape.'"

Then those who feared the LORD talked with each other, and the LORD listened and heard. A scroll of remembrance was written in his presence concerning those who feared the LORD and honored his name.

"They will be mine," says the LORD Almighty, "in the day when I make up my treasured possession. I will spare them, just as in compassion a man spares his son who serves him. And you will again see the distinction between the righteous and the wicked, between those who serve God and those who do not." (Malachi 3:6–18)

That day is coming. Will you be standing on the firm foundation of obedience to God's absolutes? Will your name be on the scroll of those who feared the Lord and honored His name? Will you be evaluated by the Lord as righteous or wicked, as serving God or not serving Him? Will you have exerted your power of one?

The decision is yours to make according to your free will and your faith.

Establishing Christ's Presence in Your World

Write down a list of twenty things that you know without a shadow of doubt.

Identify at least one area of your life in which you know that you are not trusting God to be "absolutely" on your side. Get to the core of the reason that you doubt God's ability or desire to work all things for your eternal good. Is it a matter of sin in your life? If so, repent. Is it a matter of having a false concept of the nature of God? If so, study what God's Word has to say about the nature of God and believe His Word! If your lack of trust is a matter of your wanting something that you aren't sure is God's best for you, adjust what you want!

Reflect or Discuss

- Reflect upon an incident in your life in which you came to know experientially that God's Word is true or that God's Word can be trusted. How did this experience strengthen your faith?

If God said it, God meant it. If God said He'd do it, He will. If you say something, mean it. If you say you will do something, do it. God calls us to be as trustworthy toward Him and toward others as He is toward us.

CHAPTER TWENTY-THREE

You Can Be Right Without Rage

After I had spoken one day on the subject of Daniel, a person came to me and said, "I think the Bible left something out."

"What's that?" I asked.

"The Bible forgot to say how angry Shadrach, Meshach, and Abednego were that they had been tossed into a fiery furnace. The Bible forgot to tell how ticked off Daniel was that Nebuchadnezzar was going to kill him and his friends just because the ol' king couldn't remember a dream. The Bible forgot to say how upset Daniel was that he had spent the night in a lions' den."

"Perhaps they weren't angry," I offered.

"That just isn't real!" the person said.

"The most likely reason they were not

You must rid yourselves of all such things as these: anger, rage, malice, slander, and filthy language from your lips.

(COLOSSIANS 3:8)

angry is because they knew the possible price of exercising the power of one," I said.

The truth is, most people do not believe that anger is a choice. They see anger as an automatic emotion that flows out of a person as an instinctual response, and only then does it become subject to the human will. The truth of God is this: we can choose not to be angry—especially when we take a stand.

Jesus taught this as one of his priority statements in the Sermon on the Mount: "You have heard that it was said to the people long ago, 'Do not murder, and anyone who murders will be subject to judgment.' But I tell you that anyone who is angry with his brother will be subject to judgment" (Matt. 5:21–22).

Anger, if carried to its logical and most intense conclusion, kills. It may not result in the outright murder of another person, but anger kills relationships, it kills reputations, and it kills influence. An angry attitude can keep others from receiving your message positively or acting on your behalf.

The writer of Proverbs said:

A gentle answer turns away wrath,
    but a harsh word stirs up anger.
The tongue of the wise commends knowledge,
    but the mouth of the fool gushes folly.

(PROVERBS 15:1–2)

A king's wrath is like the roar of a lion;
    he who angers him forfeits his life.
It is to a man's honor to avoid strife,
    but every fool is quick to quarrel.

(PROVERBS 20:2–3)

Angry outbursts have no benefit! People say stupid, silly things in anger. They provoke arguments that are not quickly resolved or quickly forgotten. Anger breeds resentment, bitterness, hate, and vengeance. An angry outburst may call attention to your pain, but it does nothing positive or concrete to relieve your pain!

Any time you are taking a stand for the truth of God or are advocating the right thing to do in any situation, you must control your emotions and avoid anger. Unbridled anger can negate positive power-of-one words and behaviors.

A Short Course on Anger

Let me give you a quick course in Anger 101. Anger is an emotion that every human being feels. It is the signal to our souls that something is wrong. It is the signal that says to us, "Something needs to be brought into alignment with God's commandments." Anger in itself is not a bad thing. It is like a clanging bell deep within us that calls us to wake up and take action.

Any time a person treats you in an unkind, ungodly, or unjust manner, you should feel a bit of anger.

Any time you see another person being mistreated, abused, or injured, you should feel a bit of anger.

Any time you perceive that the devil is influencing, tempting, or ensnaring a person, you should feel a bit of anger.

If you don't feel any anger at all, your heart has become hardened or your conscience seared. Ask God to restore in you a sensitivity for what is right and wrong, to rekindle a compassion in your heart for others, or to forgive you of the sin that has blinded you to the truth.

What you do when you feel that bit of anger is the critically important factor! The apostle Paul wrote, "'In your anger do not sin': Do not let the sun go down while you are still angry, and do not give the devil a foothold" (Eph. 4:26–27).

We are to channel feelings of anger into positive actions, not negative ones. There's no justification in God's Word for lashing out at another person with an angry tone of voice, or for losing our tempers when we feel that others have shown disrespect or have ignored our opinions. God empowers us to control our emotions, not to allow our emotions to control us.

The Greek language has two words for anger—the first is *thermos*. The expression of this type of anger is a quick burst, a sudden blaze that quickly dissipates. We would probably describe it as an *eruption* of anger. The second type of anger is a smoldering one—an anger that is cradled and kept warm deep within a person. It is a brooding, stewing anger.

Neither type of anger produces health and wholeness—unless they are directed at unrighteousness and not people. Only God can be angry with people.

Both types of anger kill—just in different ways and at different times.

"But I've always been hot-tempered," a person may say. "I get angry quickly and then I'm over it. That's just the way God made me."

You may be hot-tempered, but that isn't the way God made you. It's very likely the example you saw in your home when you were a child and you adopted that behavior without thinking about it. You may think that you get over your anger quickly, but whom do you damage in the process? How long does it take for the person who overheard your angry outburst to recover? What damage did you do to the child who heard your angry tirade through a closed door? What damage did you do to your own heart and cardiovascular system in your eruption of rage?

Anger always kills.

It kills innocence.

It kills feelings of love.

It kills romance.

It kills feelings of security and comfort.

It kills T-cells and causes blood clots to erupt in the veins.

Anger kills.

Cold anger—the seething, fomenting anger in a person's soul—is even more deadly than *hot anger* that spews out like a volcano. When a person stuffs the emotions of anger and does not channel it into productive and positive behavior, the rage ferments inside him. Eventually it will erupt, perhaps not in violent language or behavior, but rather in quiet and just as hurtful displays of bitterness, hatred, prejudice, mistrust, and cynicism. A great deal of criticism and sarcasm in our world today is an expression of deep-seated anger.

This type of anger also kills. It quickly turns into hatred, which is the primary motivation for murder.

Slow, seething anger can kill the degree to which other people want to hear what you have to say. It kills receptivity to your message, and if you are attempting to speak up for what you know is God's will in a particular situation, your anger can kill receptivity not only to God's commandments but to Jesus Christ. Anger repels, it does not attract.

Someone may say, "Did not God get angry at disobedience?" Yes, but God's anger is not capricious, vindictive, and self-centered, as our anger often is. God's anger is always a righteous anger.

What about Words of Contempt?

Explosive, hot-tempered anger often results in abusive expressions of contempt. Jesus said angry people are likely to say "Raca" to their brother. They are likely to dismiss their brothers as "fools" (Matt. 5:22).

The word "Raca" is not translatable. It is more of a sound than a word. Someone once said that it is a combination of "harumpfff" and "aaaargh," spoken with total disdain.

Nobody hears or heeds a person who speaks with contempt. Take a look again at the way Daniel repeatedly addressed those to whom he was called to speak God's truth. He said to Nebuchadnezzar, "You, O king, are the king of kings. The God of heaven has given you dominion and power and might and glory" (Dan. 2:37). He said to Darius, "O king, live forever!" (Dan. 6:21).

Daniel expressed no contempt for those in authority over him, even though they had made or were about to make very bad decisions! There appears to be no anger in Daniel for these emperors. He appears to have seen them as God's creation, for whom God alone was responsible, and as frail, ignorant, troubled human beings.

That's the key! Our anger is what God has built into us to fuel our response to situations—to circumstances, obstacles, bad judgments, false opinions, abusive behavior. We are not to be angry with people, but rather with their deeds.

If we approach a person with anger, contempt, or threats, we negate everything good that we hope to accomplish before we ever open our mouths.

If you recognize that you are an angry person—either quick to explode in anger or that you are harboring a deep, inner anger—ask God to forgive you, cleanse you, and teach you how to harness your anger.

Harnessing Your Anger

Jesus told His followers how they should use their anger for good.

AS A MOTIVATION TOWARD RECONCILIATION

First, your angry feelings should motivate you to seek reconciliation with the person who has wronged you, hurt someone you love, or made an ungodly decision. Acknowledge to the offending person that you are angry and tell the person why you feel the way you do—but do not speak in an angry tone. As the writer of Proverbs says, use a "gentle" voice (Prov. 15:1). Don't dismiss or put down the other person in your tone of voice. Be sincerely sorry that there is a rift between you and express genuine concern that it be healed.

Be factual and honest in telling the person how his behavior has hurt you or another person. Be forthright in telling a person how you believe his decision is going to injure a specific person or a group, community, or church. Confront the person but with a desire to be reconciled to him. Go to the person with the goal of seeing brokenness mended and the problem resolved. Go with a faith-filled expectation that bad decisions or ungodly behavior will be reversed in repentance. Go to the person seeking ways in which a wrong can be righted.

Anger estranges people from one another. Seek reconciliation. The apostle Paul wrote to the Ephesians, "Each of you must put off falsehood and speak truthfully to his neighbor, for we are all members of one body" (Eph. 4:25). Don't pretend that nothing is wrong. Don't go on as if nothing bad has happened. Confront the person, but with love and a desire to bring healing to yourself, the other person, and anybody else who may have been injured.

Use your power of one to reconcile!

AS A MOTIVATION TOWARD RESOLUTION

Second, we should seek to settle disputes without involving others and without taking legal action. This may not always be possible, but it should be our first desire and our first course of action. Go to a person with whom you have a disagreement and try to find common ground. You may not be able to convince the person to adopt your opinion or position, but do your best to speak what you believe as clearly and boldly as possible without anger. Respect the other person's right to exercise his free will and voice his opinion. Appeal to the person's sense of justice and compassion. Seek a solution that is mutually agreeable.

Use your power of one to resolve disagreements.

If you are at fault—or even if you are not at fault and the other person perceives that you are—apologize and ask forgiveness. So many times anger seethes in a heart because a person refuses to give or seek forgiveness. Forgiveness is a letting go of the dispute between you. Forgiveness is letting God decide. It is saying to another person, "Let's lay down this argument [or fight] and move forward in a way that allows us to live in peace."

The peaceful resolution may mean that you have little or nothing to do with each other in the future. But a peaceful resolution also means that you may have an opportunity for influence or genuine reconciliation in the future!

If you go to a person in anger, he will not readily accept you for a second hearing. The problem will only have grown greater.

If you go to a person with a sincere desire to seek resolution and with an attitude of forgiveness and peace, you may very well have set the stage for another encounter down the line in which your opinions or viewpoint are favorably received.

Does it really matter who asks forgiveness of whom? No.

What matters is that you let a dispute come to a resting point between you so that God has time and opportunity to work in the heart of the offending person.

Don't let anger kill a relationship.

Don't let anger kill an opportunity for you to continue to speak up for God's truth and righteousness.

Establishing Christ's Presence in Your World

Be very honest with yourself. Are you harboring anger in your heart toward another person? Do you erupt in anger at times, usually saying something you wish you could take back—not necessarily because you have spoken something that isn't true but because you have hurt another person or hurt your own chances of being heard? If so, make an appointment with a godly counselor who can help you get to the root of your anger, help you eliminate the causes of your anger if at all possible, and teach you how to harness your anger in the future.

If you have offended someone in your anger, go to that person and apologize. Seek to make amends. Ask for forgiveness and seek reconciliation.

Reflect or Discuss

- Why do we find it so difficult to ask forgiveness when we are in an estranged relationship?
- How important is forgiveness to genuine reconciliation?
- How can we become more willing to forgive quickly?
- How can we become less prone to erupting in anger quickly?

Choose to replace anger with positive action. Choose to speak words of reconciliation, reason, and resolution—and mean them from the heart.

CHAPTER TWENTY-FOUR

You Can Pray for God's Help in Times of Pressure

I am always amazed when people make prayer their last resort in times of great difficulty. God's desire is that prayer be our first resort any time we are facing a challenging question or problem.

Choose to cry out to God immediately!

Choose to get God's help quickly!

Choose to trust God to act on your behalf sooner rather than later!

When Daniel heard that a death sentence had been decreed for all the wise men in Babylon—including himself and his friends—what did he do? He immediately called his friends to urgent prayer.

When Daniel heard that Darius had issued a decree that those who prayed to any other god or person for thirty days

[Jesus said,] Watch and pray so that you will not fall into temptation. The spirit is willing, but the body is weak.

(MATTHEW 26:41)

would be thrown into a den of lions, what did he do? He immediately prayed.

When Daniel was troubled in his spirit by a disturbing dream, what did he do? He immediately asked the Lord to give him the meaning of the dream. In other words, he prayed, even in his sleep.

Our Hesitation in Praying

Why is it that we hesitate in asking for the Lord's help or wisdom immediately? There seem to be at least three reasons:

1. We think we can solve the problem in our own strength.
2. We think we can resolve the riddle in our own intellect.
3. We think we can change another person's opinion or attitude.

Furthermore, we think God expects us to solve our own problems, come up with our own solutions, and have enough persuasive charm to get others to agree with us. We think incorrectly!

In truth, you can't do anything in your own strength. It is God who gives you life, moment by moment and breath by breath. It is God who gives you creative ideas and innovative insights. It is God who melts the heart of an obstinate, mean, or calloused person to hear what you have to say and receive it as wisdom. It is God who pricks the heart of an unyielding person to be receptive to the work He desires to do in his or her life.

In truth, God does not expect you to act independently of Him. He not only wants you to rely upon Him fully for strength, wisdom, and godly attitudes and behavior, He commands you to trust in Him.

Daniel understood very clearly that God was his source of strength and wisdom. Read again what he said in praise to the God of heaven:

Wisdom and power are his.
He changes times and seasons;
  he sets up kings and deposes them.

He gives wisdom to the wise
  and knowledge to the discerning.
He reveals deep and hidden things;
  he knows what lies in darkness.
(DANIEL 2:20–22)

  God has made it very clear throughout His Word that He wants us to turn to Him and receive His counsel and strength. He wants us to rely upon Him for help. Any power of one that you may have flows from total dependency on the Lord. Just read some of what He has commanded:

Call upon me in the day of trouble;
  I will deliver you, and you will honor me.
(PSALM 50:15)

He will call upon me, and I will answer him;
  I will be with him in trouble,
  I will deliver him and honor him.
With long life will I satisfy him
  and show him my salvation.
(PSALM 91:15–16)

"I know the plans I have for you," declares the LORD, "plans to prosper you and not to harm you, plans to give you hope and a future. Then you will call upon me and come and pray to me, and I will listen to you. You will seek me and find me when you seek me with all your heart. I will be found by you," declares the LORD. (Jeremiah 29:11–14)

If my people, who are called by my name, will humble themselves and pray and seek my face and turn from their wicked ways, then will I hear from heaven and will forgive their sin and will heal their land. (2 Chronicles 7:14)

When Solomon was crowned king, he offered a thousand burnt offerings to the Lord on the altar at Gibeon and asked, "Give your servant a discerning heart to govern your people and to distinguish between right and wrong" (1 Kings 3:9). The Bible tells us that the Lord was pleased that Solomon had asked for this. God said to him,

> Since you have asked for this and not for long life or wealth for yourself, nor have asked for the death of your enemies, but for discernment in administering justice, I will do what you have asked. I will give you a wise and discerning heart, so that there will never have been anyone like you, nor will there ever be. Moreover, I will give you what you have not asked for—both riches and honor—so that in your lifetime you will have no equal among kings. (1 Kings 3:11–13)

When Esther was facing the biggest challenge of her young life and the lives of all her people hung in the balance, she called upon Mordecai to lead people in fasting and praying on her behalf. She and her maids also fasted and prayed. Esther was seeking God's favor, wisdom, and courage. She got what she was seeking (Esther 4:15–16).

Solomon and Esther were both people of tremendous influence by reason of their positions—one a king, the other a queen. Yet even they turned to prayer and voiced their reliance upon the Lord before acting on their power-of-one desires.

When Jesus, our ultimate model for the power of one, was facing the greatest hours of agony in His life, He went to a garden called Gethsemane and He prayed. Jesus was seeking God's will, and His prayer said it all: "My Father, if it is possible, may this cup be taken from me. Yet not as I will, but as you will" (Matt. 26:39). Jesus received the strength to endure the cross that was before Him.

After Peter and John had healed a blind man and exalted Jesus as Savior, then were arrested and called before the Sanhedrin to explain their actions, they were released with a stern warning that they were to cease and desist from all ministry efforts. What did they do? They immediately went to their fellow believers in Jerusalem and reported what had happened. And then, the Bible tells us, "they raised their voices together in prayer to God" (Acts 4:24). What did they pray? They prayed for greater boldness in ministry!

They said, "Now, Lord, consider their threats and enable your servants to speak your word with great boldness. Stretch out your hand to heal and perform miraculous signs and wonders through the name of your holy servant Jesus." The Bible tells us that after they prayed, the place where they were meeting was "shaken." They were filled with the Holy Spirit and "spoke the word of God boldly" (Acts 4:29–31).

Are you praying today for God to give you clear discernment about right and wrong, and about the decisions you should make or the actions you should take?

Are you praying today for God's wisdom and favor as you seek to go to those who have the authority to bring about the justice or solutions you seek?

Are you praying today for God's will to be accomplished in you and through you?

Are you praying today for God's boldness — and for God to use you in any way He desires to establish His plans and purposes on this earth?

Follow the examples of these Bible role models in praying for power-of-one wisdom, discernment, courage, and effectiveness.

Three Guidelines for Your Prayer

The Bible gives us three guidelines for our prayers in times of trouble.

I. PRAY WITH FAITH

First, we must believe and not doubt when we pray (James 1:6). In order to pray with great faith, we must be 100 percent certain that we are asking the Lord to do something that is totally in keeping with His commandments and His plans and purposes for mankind. If we know that God desires to accomplish something, we are to pray with boldness that He will do it.

Many times, God waits for a person or a group of people to invite Him into a situation to do His work—to heal, deliver, save souls, bring about a revival, renew hearts, or reconcile relationships. God honors the free will He has given us, all the time hoping we will use that free will to give Him free rein!

2. PRAY WITH OTHERS

Second, join with others to pray about what concerns you individually and collectively. Daniel didn't pray alone. Moses didn't pray alone—he frequently went into the presence of the Lord with another person, sometimes Joshua, sometimes Aaron. Jesus didn't pray alone. He especially asked Peter, James, and John to be with Him numerous times in prayer situations, and especially so in the Garden of Gethsemane. Peter and John didn't pray alone. They sought out other believers to pray and agree with them.

If you are facing a difficult situation, seek out a group of people who will support you in prayer and who will believe with you for God's will to be accomplished.

3. PRAY FOR GOD TO GET GLORY

Third, pray for the promises and desires of God to be fulfilled so that God gets all the glory. We sometimes fail to see answers to our prayers because we ask amiss. We ask for our own satisfaction, or we ask out of greed or selfishness. Make sure your prayers are for the good of all concerned. Give God full credit for the victories He allows you to experience and the goals He allows you to accomplish.

Not long ago a person came to me and told me this story. A group of people had joined together to pray to and believe in God to close down a "strip joint" in a nice residential neighborhood of their city. The group had already gone to the city council with a petition. They had walked a picket line in front of the establishment. They had sought out an appointment with the owner of the establishment, but he had refused to meet with them. Nothing they had tried worked. They began to pray in earnest.

The man telling me this story said, "We met on three occasions to pray very specifically for God to close this business, and frankly, we were getting a little discouraged. We had been very careful not to broadcast to others that we were praying, since we were concerned that people would think we were doing that just so we could take the credit later. At least that's what we told ourselves. I think the truth was that we were a little fearful after a month of prayer that God wasn't going to answer us in the way we wanted."

"How long did you pray?" I asked.

"Well, that's the interesting thing," this man said. "After the third time we prayed, one of the men in the group said, 'I think the Lord is telling me that we are to stop praying and start trusting Him to act. We are to stand in faith, believing that God has heard our prayer and is going to resolve this problem in His way and in His timing.' We all felt an agreement with that, so we stopped meeting together to pray. Occasionally we'd see one another and say, 'I'm still believing.' But that's all."

"What happened?" I asked.

"Exactly one year after our first prayer meeting, the state announced that it was going to widen a freeway through a section of our city. The widening project was going to mean the elimination of a number of businesses to the east and west of the freeway. This business was on the list to go!"

"Did that happen?" I asked.

"Not only did it happen," this man said, "but the owner of the place announced that he wasn't going to reopen anywhere else. He was going to retire."

"What a great outcome!" I said.

"Oh, there's one more thing," this man said. "We've met three times again as a group to pray that every person who worked in that place, including the owner, will get saved. And we're believing!"

Trust God for Your Good Outcome!

Continually look toward the Lord as you pray. Look to Him for guidance about *what* to pray.

Look to Him for direction about *who* needs your prayers.

Look to Him for guidance about *when* and *how* you should speak or act.

Look to Him even for the faith you need to believe that He hears and answers your prayers!

Look especially to Him with praise when the answers come, knowing that they are for your eternal benefit and that He is working all things for good, according to His purposes (Rom. 8:28).

Look to the Lord with thanksgiving that He invites you to participate with Him in blessing this world. He wants you to have a part in His miracles. He wants you to win souls for Jesus. He wants you to succeed in prayer!

Look to the Lord for a miraculous, victorious, superlative outcome!

Are you facing a tough time today?

Pray.

Establishing Christ's Presence in Your World

Write down the names of ten people for whom you know with absolute certainty that God desires you to pray.

Write down the names of five situations or problems about which you know that God desires for you to pray.

Then start praying, alone and with others. Pray with boldness and faith. Pray that God will act and that all the glory for the outcome will go to Him. Pray for guidance as you pray, that you might pray with wisdom, according to God's will, and for the fulfillment of God's purposes in your own life and the lives of others.

Don't stop praying until God answers you.

Reflect or Discuss

- What does it mean to humble oneself to pray? How important is it that our first prayer to the Lord always be a prayer that God will forgive our sins?

Pray first. Then do whatever the Lord directs you to do as you pray.

CHAPTER TWENTY-FIVE

You Can Pray Your Way Through Persecution

When we pray and God immediately answers our prayers in the way we desire, we are ecstatic! The answered prayer is like a shot of adrenaline for our faith.

When we pray and God answers our prayers in the way we desire over a period of weeks or months, we tend to be less ecstatic, but we are overjoyed when the answer finally comes. We pat ourselves on the back for having persevered in prayer. Our faith is deepened.

When we pray and God does not seem to hear us, or He is very slow in answering our prayers, we wonder if God has heard us. We sometimes find ourselves questioning ourselves and our faith. We question at times whether God loves us.

The truth of God's Word is that God

[Jesus said,] When you pray, go into your room, close the door and pray to your Father, who is unseen. Then your Father, who sees what is done in secret, will reward you.
(MATTHEW 6:6)

hears every prayer of those who trust him (Ps. 91:15). He hears us each time we pray. And He responds to prayer.

God may not respond in the way we desire. His answers may come in a way that we had not anticipated. But God always responds to prayer, and He always responds to prayer with our eternal benefit in mind.

Nobody knows the true beginning from the ending of any life story, any problem, or any opportunity. We take God's promises, God's commands, and God's imparting of faith to our hearts as evidence that God is at work in our lives, even if we cannot see where God may be leading us or what God may be doing on our behalf (2 Cor. 5:7; Heb. 11:1).

Only God sees the big picture from an eternal perspective.

Only God knows the perfect timing for a prayer to be answered in a way that we recognize as an answer to prayer.

Only God has the perfect method or avenue for answering our prayers.

We need to acknowledge with our faith that God is never late, and never early. There have been times when I have hoped against hope that God would show up early—that we'd have all the resources we needed before a project began, that we'd have total healing before the surgeon picked up a scalpel, or that the phone would ring before I had to make a call. God has a perfect timing for everything He does and only He knows it.

If we truly are to be effective as power-of-one Christians, we must trust God completely in which prayers He answers with "Yes," the methods associated with God's answers, and the timing of God's answers.

We also need to acknowledge that God's ways are higher than our ways. I fly a great deal, both in the United States and internationally, and a person gets a distinct perspective on the earth, and on life, from looking out the window of an airplane. It isn't the same perspective the person has when he is stuck in a traffic jam on a city's busy freeways, or even the same perspective a person has out on a country lane looking up at the sky. God sees things from His vantage point in heaven. He knows all the people who will be impacted by an answered prayer. He knows how the answered prayer fits into His eternal plan. And He crafts precisely the right method for answering a prayer.

We cannot see everything God sees.

We cannot know everything God knows.

We cannot truly know what is best for us, even though we seem so sure at times that we know not only what is best for ourselves but best for other people!

Throughout the Bible we find numerous examples of methods and means that God used to deliver or provide for His people. Only once, however, do we find that God enabled a person to sling a stone at a giant and bring about a mighty military and spiritual victory. Only once do we find a man hitting a body of water with a rod and the result being parted waters and ground dry enough to walk on. Only once do we find three men thrown into a fiery furnace or a man thrown into a den of lions, all of them to emerge from these death chambers alive. Only once do we find Jesus spitting on clay and applying it to a blind man's eyes to bring healing. Only once do we find a man rising from the dead in a resurrection that involved no other human being, only God's sovereign intervention.

God made you as a distinctive, unique person, placing you in a distinct time in history and in a specific place.

God uses you in a distinctive, unique way. He has given you natural and spiritual gifts in a combination that is uniquely your own.

God deals with you in a distinctive, unique way and He answers your prayers in a way that is distinctive and unique!

Don't look for your answer to prayer to come the same way it came for your pastor or neighbor or best friend.

Don't look for your answer to prayer to come in the way you think it should come or will come.

Do look, however, for God to act on your behalf! God's promise to us is that the answer to our prayer will always be for our ultimate good. The Bible tells us:

"For my thoughts are not your thoughts,
    neither are your ways my ways,"
    declares the LORD.
"As the heavens are higher than the earth,
    so are my ways higher than your ways
    and my thoughts than your thoughts.
As the rain and the snow
    come down from heaven,
and do not return to it
    without watering the earth
and making it bud and flourish,
    so that it yields seed for the sower and bread for the eater,
so is my word that goes out from my mouth:
    It will not return to me empty,
but will accomplish what I desire
    and achieve the purpose for which I sent it."

(ISAIAH 55:8–11)

Note in this promise that God tells us He has a purpose that is greater than our purposes, which we often limit to the meeting of our own needs and desires. God does what is best for the whole of His plan, and the whole of His people. Note also that God always accomplishes His purpose. His answers to us always bring about a multiplying effect that provides a blessing not only for us and our families, but for others in the body of Christ.

Think higher!

Begin to see your problem or challenge from God's perspective.

Begin to anticipate that what God is going to do will truly be immeasurably more than anything you have thus far asked or imagined (Eph. 3:20).

It is especially important—and also especially difficult—to continue to pray this way when you are under persecution or when God's answers seem to be long in coming. You may not know exactly when God has promised to turn your situation around or bring the breakthrough you desire. Keep praying! Your answer just may be closer than you think. And even if not, your prayer is the right thing to do to bring God's fulfillment and joy to your life.

Daniel's Sixty-Seven-Year Prayer Meeting

Daniel knew what it was to live in persecution and in captivity. Although he rose to great prominence and power in Babylon, his power was not unlimited. Daniel was never a free man. He never had the opportunity, after he was taken captive, to make a sacrifice to Jehovah God. He never had the opportunity to pack his bags and leave Babylon for a return trip to Jerusalem. He never had the opportunity to openly join others in worship or to celebrate the Jewish feasts and traditions.

As far as we know from the Bible account, Daniel may not have had any contact with Jews from his personal family, or even Jews who were strangers, once he arrived in Babylon, other than his three friends who were taken into captivity for the king's service at the same time he was.

Daniel lived in spiritual isolation. He lived as a captive in a foreign land. He lived a very limited and confined life.

For sixty-seven years, Daniel had worked under an assumed name, Belteshazzar, the name the Babylonians had given to him. He had survived death threats, attempted political schemes to remove him from power, and a night spent with some big cats that could have ripped him to shreds and called him an appetizer. Not only had he faced these high-drama moments, but Daniel had worked day in and day out, week in and week out, month in and month out, year in and year out in service to his captors. He had been loyal to them and not been at all negligent in his duties, working well past retirement age to his eighties. He had worked for several emperors but without any assurance or even a hint from any of them that they might one day send the Jews back to Jerusalem.

Furthermore, Daniel possibly was praying on behalf of people who were not praying for themselves, didn't know Daniel was praying for them, and could not have cared less. There's no indication whatsoever that others in Babylon were praying as Daniel was praying.

Nevertheless. . . .

And "nevertheless" is a key word! It means "even so, in spite of, although all facts would indicate otherwise."

Nevertheless, Daniel believed in an unlimited God. He believed in a God who always kept His promises. And he believed that one of those promises was on the near horizon, at last.

After living in Babylon for sixty-seven years, Daniel consulted his calendar and began to pray with renewed fervor for the fulfillment of God's promise. The Bible tells us:

> In the first year of Darius son of Xerxes (a Mede by descent), who was made ruler over the Babylonian kingdom — in the first year of his reign, I, Daniel, understood from the Scriptures, according to the word of the LORD given to Jeremiah the prophet, that the desolation of Jerusalem would last seventy years. So I turned to the Lord God and pleaded with him in prayer and petition, in fasting, and in sackcloth and ashes. (Daniel 9:1–3)

Daniel knew that Jeremiah had prophesied that the captivity in Babylon would last for seventy years (Jer. 25:12). Only a couple of years were left! But Daniel not only knew about the seventy years, he knew the fullness of the prophecies of Jeremiah. Jeremiah had prophesied that Jerusalem would be badly damaged and desolate (Jer. 25), the Jews would be taken into captivity and would serve Nebuchadnezzar (Jer. 27), and that the Lord would one day allow His people to return to Jerusalem and restore to them the lands of Israel and Judah (Jer. 30). He knew that at the end of seventy years, Babylon would be destroyed and made desolate forever. God had said, "I will bring upon that land all the things I have spoken against it. . . . They themselves will be enslaved by many nations and great kings; I will repay them according to their deeds and the work of their hands" (Jer. 25:13–14).

Although it may have been strongly indicated and believed,

nothing in the prophecies of Jeremiah said that on the stroke of the beginning of the seventieth year of captivity, all of the Jews would be allowed to take caravans back across the deserts and mountains to Jerusalem.

Daniel knew the promise. He didn't know the precise timing or method.

This is a critically important point for you and me as we face persecutions and troubled times in our lives. We know that God will prevail in accomplishing all He has promised in His Word. But just *when* and *how* are questions for which we don't have answers.

Faith that Endures

After a lesson on prayer a person once said to me, "Pastor, God sure asks a lot. He reminds me of my mother."

"Your mother?" I said. "What do you mean?"

"My mother used to tell me things and when I asked her why, she'd say, 'Because I said so.' When I asked her when, she'd say, 'When the time is right.' When I asked her how she was going to do something, she'd say, 'I'm going to do it the right way.' When I asked her to tell me what she meant when she said she had a nice surprise for me, she'd say, 'You'll like it when you get it.' God reminds me of my mother!"

In many ways, God does ask us to trust Him completely and solely because He is God and we aren't. He asks us to rely on Him because He says that He is trustworthy and unchanging. That's what faith is all about. It's clinging to God's promises and trusting in God's trustworthy nature even when we have questions about why God wants something, how God will do something, when God will act, or what exactly God is going to do.

The apostle Paul said we walk by faith, not by sight (2 Cor. 5:7).

I once watched a blind man who had tremendous mobility skills. He could walk right up to the edge of a platform and speak, with the entire audience holding its breath in fear that if he took one more step he'd fall into the orchestra pit. He never took that extra step. I watched this man talk to other people—he seemed to look them in the eye just as a man would do if he could see clearly.

I asked someone how he did what he did and this person replied, "He goes out onto a stage long before an event and counts the steps to the edge of the stage. He practices listening to people of various heights so he knows where to look based upon the directions their voices are coming from."

Then, knowing that I am a pastor, this person added, "He has a very practical definition of what it means to walk by faith. He believes it means having faith that the stage manager isn't going to move the edge of the stage and that God will help him remember how many steps he can take!"

Our evidence is God's Word—which is filled with examples of God's trustworthiness. Our evidence is a look back into the past of our own lives—which is also filled with examples of God's trustworthiness. Our evidence may be looking at examples in the lives of people we know, hear about, or read about—every life has examples of God's trustworthiness. Faith is taking those examples personally and believing that who God is will be who God continues to be.

If God ever was a Provider, He is still a Provider and will provide now.

If God ever was a Protector, He is still a Protector and will protect now.

If God ever was a Problem-Solver, He is still a Problem-Solver and will solve the current problem.

Choose to trust God to *be* God in *your* life today as you step out to be a power-of-one Christian.

Establishing Christ's Presence in Your World

Write down the problem that concerns you the most.

Next to the name of this problem, write down three words that describe the nature of the problem.

Next to each of these descriptive words, write down the name of God, or the attribute of God that is directly related.

For example, if your problem is an edict from the company that you are going to be required to work every other Sunday morning, the words you use to describe that problem might be: unfair practice, mean-spirited supervisor, and against-the-Bible demand (requiring a person to work violates God's command to keep the Sabbath). The words about God's nature that you might then write next to these descriptions might be:

unfair practice — God is just
mean-spirited supervisor — God is loving
against-the-Bible demand — God is holy

Then write down what you believe the God you have just described might ask you to do or say. In the example given, a just, loving, holy God may ask you to speak to those in upper management, appealing to them with a loving attitude to do what is just, allowing workers who want to have Sunday mornings off the privilege of having Sunday mornings off and working longer weekday hours or a Saturday shift instead.

Reflect or Discuss

- How difficult is it to be patient in a society that wants instant everything?
- How difficult is it to step back and see a problem from an eternal, heavenly perspective?
- In what ways have you personally learned that God is trustworthy? (Reflect on two or three specific experiences.)

The Lord is the *only* One who knows the best answer, the best timing, and the best method.

CHAPTER TWENTY-SIX

You Can Pray Effectively

Many people today don't seem to think that their prayers matter. They don't consider themselves to be great prayer warriors. As one person said to me not long ago, "Prayer warrior? Not me! When it comes to prayer, I feel as if I'm a prayer wimp."

Even people who believe in prayer and who have confidence that God hears and answers their prayers don't always think of themselves as being effective in prayer.

To be effective means to get results. It means to help make things happen for the furtherance of God's purposes.

The Bible tells us that the person who is effective is a "righteous person." A righteous person is in right standing with God.

The prayer of a righteous man is powerful and effective.
(JAMES 5:16)

That means the person has accepted Jesus as his or her personal Savior and stands in a position of forgiveness before God. It means the person is yielding to the leadership of the Holy Spirit in his or her life and is seeking to obey God in all things. It means the person wants what is right according to the Word of God—he or she wants to see God's truth and God's will established on this earth.

In talking about the effectiveness of prayer, James also said, "Elijah was a man just like us. He prayed earnestly that it would not rain, and it did not rain on the land for three and a half years. Again he prayed, and the heavens gave rain, and the earth produced its crops" (James 5:17–18). Elijah certainly was effective. If you go back into the Old Testament and read about Elijah, you'll find these words: "After a long time, in the third year, the word of the LORD came to Elijah: 'Go and present yourself to Ahab, and I will send rain on the land'" (1 Kings 18:1). Elijah had no doubt about the right thing. He prayed fully within the truth of what God had already revealed He was going to do.

Daniel's Prayer

Daniel was also a man in right standing with God. How, then, did Daniel pray?

A PREAMBLE OF PRAISE

Daniel praised God. He prayed to "the great and awesome God, who keeps his covenant of love with all who love him and obey his commands" (Dan. 9:4). He acknowledged God as absolutely righteous, but also merciful and forgiving.

Never lose sight of the truth that God doesn't owe you anything. You owe everything to God. God is under no obligation to do your bidding. You are under every obligation to do His. Praise God continually and in all situations solely because He is God and He is worthy to be praised. Regardless of what you are facing, or the reasons for it, God is the one to whom we pray, "Yours is the kingdom, and the power, and the glory!"

A CONFESSION OF SIN

Daniel confessed that Israel had sinned. He didn't try to dismiss, justify, or sidestep the fact that Israel had made a grave error, not just once or for a short period of time, but for generations. The reason for the captivity, as Jeremiah had prophesied for more than twenty-three years, was the sin of the Jews in not obeying God. Daniel stated up front in his prayer, "We have sinned and done wrong. We have been wicked and have rebelled; we have turned away from your commands and laws. We have not listened to your servants the prophets, who spoke in your name to our kings, our princes and our fathers, and to all the people in the land" (Dan. 9:5–6).

When you go to God in prayer, don't play the blame game when it comes to your problem. Acknowledge any element of sin or misdoing—intentional or unintentional—related to the situation or circumstance. It's so easy to say in the face of tremendous societal woes, "I had nothing to do with this. It's so-and-so's fault." You may think the government officials are at fault, the corporate leaders are at fault, the religious leaders are at fault, or the justice system is at fault.

But . . .

Who elected the government officials? Who stood by and said nothing as law after law was passed, undermining the morality and ethical foundation of the nation? Who reelected the very government officials who were passing those laws?

Who went to work for the corporation that mismanaged funds? Who invested in that corporation? Who failed to invest at all?

Who supported the corrupt ministry or gave allegiance to a heretical church or its leadership? Who allowed part of his tithes and offerings to go to a national church organization that does not believe in the truth of the Bible or the distinctiveness of Jesus as Savior?

Who sat idly and silently by as decisions were made, leaders were chosen, policies were enacted, and questions were raised?

Who failed to pray for those in authority?

Who failed to speak up for truth in the conversation by the water cooler, failed to show up for the shareholders' meeting to ask questions, or failed to vote in the last school board election?

Who had potential power-of-one influence and failed to exert it?

AN APPEAL FOR MERCY

Daniel appealed to God's mercy. He said, "O Lord, in keeping with all your righteous acts, turn away your anger and your wrath from Jerusalem. . . . For your sake, O Lord, look with favor on our desolate sanctuary. . . . We do not make requests of you because we are righteous, but because of your great mercy" (Dan. 9:16–18).

A PETITION FOR GOD TO ACT

Daniel very specifically asked the Lord to take action: "O Lord, listen! O Lord, forgive! O Lord, hear and act! For your sake, O my God, do not delay, because your city and your people bear your Name" (Dan. 9:19).

Notice three things about this prayer: 1) Daniel did not pray that he personally would be allowed to return to Jerusalem. 2) Daniel did not even pray that other captives or their descendants in Babylon would be allowed to return in the next three years. 3) Daniel did not pray that his life would be spared if Babylon was overrun by enemies and made desolate.

Daniel prayed for the Lord to show Himself strong so that the Lord might receive glory on this earth.

When we begin to pray as Daniel prayed, persecution and troubled times take on a whole new meaning! God does not call us to pray that our persecution will end so we can live more comfortably, or that a law might be passed so we will receive greater personal benefit, or that our particular pet cause might be enacted or upheld so that our organization can be given credit. Rather, we are to pray that God will act in a way that brings God the greatest glory and in a way that is the most profound witness that Jesus is the Christ, the Son of the Living God!

Our society is in a mess today.

Christians are going to suffer more and more if that mess is allowed to continue or grow.

God has called us to pray. If we truly want to be power-of-one Christians, we need to learn to pray as Daniel prayed.

We must pray with praise on our lips, a confession of our own fault in allowing the mess to develop, and with a petition that God will act in the way that accomplishes God's purposes and brings God glory. And then, we must listen very closely to what God may lead us to say or do. God uses individual people to accomplish His purposes. Be willing to be used.

What About Praying for Personal Needs in Times of Trouble?

This is not to say at all that we should never ask God to meet our personal needs for safety, provision, or justice. Jesus told a parable addressing that very issue:

> In a certain town there was a judge who neither feared God nor cared about men. And there was a widow in that town who kept coming to him with the plea, "Grant me justice against my adversary."
>
> For some time he refused. But finally he said to himself, "Even though I don't fear God or care about men, yet because this widow keeps bothering me, I will see that she gets justice, so that she won't eventually wear me out with her coming!" (Luke 18:2–5)

Jesus went on to say, "Listen to what the unjust judge says. And will not God bring about justice for his chosen ones, who cry out to him day and night? Will he keep putting them off? I tell you, he will see that they get justice, and quickly" (Luke 18:6–8).

Jesus also encouraged His followers to keep praying and believing with faith. He said as His conclusion to this parable, "When the Son of Man comes, will he find faith on the earth?" (Luke 18:8).

It's not wrong to ask God to meet your needs.

It's not wrong to ask God to give you the desires of your heart.

It's not wrong to ask God for your persecution to end and for justice to be done.

What is wrong is praying with a self-centered or sinful attitude. Ask God to do *His* will. His will will be for your good, and for the good of others as well.

Praying the Will of God

How can you be assured that you are praying for *God's* will, and not your own, to be done? Jesus said that we are to seek first the things of God and that God would respond by taking care of our needs. Immerse yourself in the Word of God. Discover what God desires to do for humanity and for lost souls. Discover how God wants to bless those who are obedient to Him.

Ask God to send laborers into the harvest, healers to the sick, and comforters to the dying. Ask Him to send teachers to the ignorant, preachers to the rebellious, and counselors to those who need wisdom. Ask Him to show you ways in which you might meet the practical needs of those who are hurting—providing food for the hungry, shelter for the homeless, encouragement for the discouraged, and the gospel to those who have never heard it. Ask how you might speak up or take action in a way that will bless people and bring glory to God.

Second, as you read God's Word and study it, ask the Lord to give you a greater awareness of specific promises that He wants you as an individual to pray about and believe for. Daniel may have prayed the prayer we find in Daniel 9 for six decades. We don't know. We do know that Daniel felt a quickening in his heart to pray during the first year Darius was ruler over Babylon. Daniel said he "understood from the Scriptures" (Dan. 9:2). He appears to have had new insight into what God had promised.

Look for that to happen in your life. As you read the promises of God—which are sometimes for everyone, sometimes conditional, and sometimes for certain people or limited times—ask God for insight into which of His promises apply to your situation and your life right now. Pray that God's promises will be fulfilled according to His Word.

Finally, as you pray, never lose sight of this truth: "Let us not become weary in doing good, for at the proper time we will reap a harvest if we do not give up" (Gal. 6:9). Continue to pray, knowing that at God's appointed time, your harvest will come.

Establishing Christ's Presence in Your World

Find the promise in God's Word that you know with certainty applies to your situation or circumstance. Pray for God to fulfill that promise.

What do you believe—firmly, without doubt—God desires to do for you and others in the current time of persecution or trouble that you are facing? Write down that prayer request. Ask the Lord to confirm to you in ways only He can that this truly is something He desires for you.

Reflect or Discuss

- What changes happen in the human heart when a person prays that God will do whatever is necessary to bring Him the greatest glory—rather than pray that God will act to bring the person the greatest benefit or recognition?

Seek to be in right standing with your unlimited Creator, who has unlimited and creative ways of answering your "right" prayers.

CHAPTER TWENTY-SEVEN

You Can Trust God to Help You Make Right Decisions

Many people say that they want to "live right" or "do what is right." We know as Christians that the right way to live is to live in obedience to God's commandments—to love God with all of our hearts, minds, and strength, and to love our neighbors as ourselves. Any habit or pattern of behavior in our lives that displays obedience to these commands is a *right* thing to do!

What does it mean, however, to make a right choice? When we reach a crossroads in life, how can we know whether it is right for us to turn left, turn right, go forward, or perhaps just sit and rest for a while at the stoplight?

If you do whatever I command you and walk in my ways and do what is right in my eyes . . . I will be with you.
(1 KINGS 11:38)

Asking the Right Questions

Very often making the right choice or decision is a process that involves answering one or more of three questions:

Question #1: Do I understand what is at stake in making this decision? Do I truly have a grasp of what God lays out as the consequences associated with each of the various options before me?

Question #2: Is this choice related to a fleeting or durable situation? Is it a choice that impacts today, or the rest of my life? Is it a decision that will determine only what I do this coming month, or a decision that will set a direction for many years to come?

Question #3: Is this decision born out of a God-given vision for my life? Is the decision one that will impact the fulfillment of that vision, or is it a choice or decision based upon what I currently find enticing? Is it a decision that must be made, or is it a decision that might be made? Is it a choice I feel compelled to make before the Lord, or a choice I think is possibly advantageous?

Daniel's Desire to Understand

Repeatedly in Daniel's visions and dreams toward the end of his life, Daniel went to the Lord to ask God to give him discernment. At times, he didn't need to overtly ask for an interpretation — the Lord saw that he was perplexed, or in mourning, and the Lord sent an answer.

After Daniel had prayed to the Lord to ask Him to listen, forgive, and act on behalf of the Jews in Babylonian captivity and for the sake of Jerusalem, he suddenly had a vision of a messenger from the Lord named Gabriel! The Bible tells us that this happened while he was "speaking and praying, confessing my sin and the sin of my people . . . and making my request" (Dan. 9:20). Gabriel came to Daniel, saying, "I have come to give you insight and understanding. As soon as you began to pray, an answer was given, which I have come to tell you, for you are highly esteemed" (Dan. 9:22–23).

Look for what happened to Daniel to happen in your life. As you praise God, confess your sins before God, and ask God for the things you need or want, *listen*!

First, listen to your own voice. What is your tone of voice? What are you really asking for? What is it that you are telling God you want . . . and for what reasons? Very often when we begin to analyze our own prayers, we come away thinking, *I really didn't know that is what I wanted. I really didn't know I was feeling that way about this. I didn't really understand the fullness of what I have as a desire of my heart.*

Second, listen after you have prayed to what God may want to say to you. Don't be too quick to get up from your knees and go about your daily tasks. Be open and receptive to things that the Lord may bring to your mind, or to the Scriptures that He may call you to read again or study anew.

A man once said to me, "Pastor, I'm not sure I want to wait to listen to what God has to say. I'm too scared that He might say, 'Oh George (not his real name), stop whining and get on with it,' or 'Hey George, how many times are you going to ask for this before you realize My answer is no?'"

He wasn't kidding. I said, "George, the Lord may also say to you, 'Listen up, George, here's what's really at stake. Here's how Answer A would impact your world, and here's how Answer B would impact it. Now which do you really want?'"

George appeared stunned. "I never thought of that," he said.

"God might also say, 'George, you don't have a full grasp of the consequences associated with what you are asking. Let me show you that if I answer precisely what you have prayed for, you are going to be miserable.'"

George thought this over for a few moments and then said, "I guess I've always thought that God was going to pull me up short and say, 'You are asking for the wrong thing.' I never thought that prayer might be something of a dialogue, with God giving me an opportunity to alter my requests."

George had a wonderful insight that day. It changed the way he prayed.

God wants to inform you about what you are praying. He wants you to pray in the Spirit and with understanding. The apostle Paul stated that one of the main purposes of his ministry was so that the people he taught might be "encouraged in heart and united in love, so that they may have the full riches of complete understanding" (Col. 2:2).

If you don't have a firm grasp of what might be fully at stake in your taking a stand for the truth or for doing what is right in a particular situation, ask the Lord to reveal to you the full ramifications of your choices, words, and actions. The choices you make not only impact your life—they impact the lives of others, perhaps *many* others.

Know what you are getting into. Know what you might expect. Know what to believe for!

Fleeting or Durable?

In the world of finances, investors often speak about "short-term" and "long-term" investments. In the world of gambling, gamblers speak about knowing when to "hold 'em" and when to "fold 'em." In the world of politics, men and women speak of decisions that will be a "quick fix" or "impact the next generation."

When we pray, we need to have an awareness of whether we are praying for a short-term goal or an eternal goal.

For example, asking the Lord to help you get through traffic so you can get to an important appointment on time can seem like a short-term goal. On the other hand, if you are always late for appointments, you perhaps need to be praying that God will help you manage your time better and make changes so that you don't miss important appointments or sully your reputation as a person who has little regard for others. If you have an awareness that your appointment is the time for a make-or-break decision, your prayers will also reflect the fact that you see this appointment as a key step toward a long-range goal.

Always be sensitive to the nature of your conversations, and especially to statements that might be overheard and misconstrued or be quoted by someone in the media. Don't say things you don't mean. Don't say things in an offhanded way, thinking nobody is paying close attention. Weigh your words and guard your speech. What you say in the casual moment might have serious long-term consequences!

On the other hand, don't let a short-term failure discourage you. Every successful person has made mistakes and will continue to make mistakes. The difference between those who succeed and those who don't is very often this: a successful person picks himself up after a failure, asks for God's forgiveness, and moves on. Troubles and failures are often fleeting moments in a more durable track record of success.

Part of a Vision or a Whim?

If you don't have a vision for why you are on this earth or about what God desires for you to be or accomplish in your life, ask God to give you such a vision! Ask Him to show you your talents and gifts. Ask Him how you might develop them so they are finely honed and ready for service. Ask Him to reveal to you what He desires for you to do with those gifts—generally speaking, that will be a way of using those gifts in service to others.

A young woman once said to me, "Now that I'm finished with college, I'm not sure what I should do. There are so many choices! So many opportunities! There are so many things I'd like to do, it's hard for me to determine what God wants me to do."

That's a position that many people, not just recent college graduates, find themselves in. The only way you can discern what God desires for you to do is to evaluate the opportunities that come your way by asking:

- Is this just fun for a little while, or fulfilling for a lifetime?
- Is this something I can build upon, or something that runs out, is a dead end, or has no potential?
- Is this something that could keep me from doing what is really valuable, eternal, or important?
- Does this sidetrack me, or is it part of the main track?

Ask God to help you answer these questions honestly and fully.

Write Down God's Vision for Your Life

Once you have a clear vision about who you are and what you are to do with your life, write it down. God wrote the commandments He gave to Moses (Exod. 34:1). The Lord told the prophet Jeremiah to "write in a book all the words I have spoken to you" (Jer. 30:2). There's great power in writing down what you know to be God's vision for your life. A written statement gives you a reference point — in the days and years ahead, it can give you focus, direction, and purpose. It also gives you a very clear way of evaluating key choices and decisions.

Does a particular choice further the accomplishment of God's vision for your life? Or does it send you on a time-wasting, resource-wasting detour?

Is a particular decision in line with the fulfillment of your life's purpose? Or does it compromise your ability to fulfill that purpose?

Ask God periodically if He desires to refocus the vision He has given you, or if He desires for you to apply your gifts to a new challenge or project. The overall vision of God for your life isn't likely to change, but the details of it may.

In Daniel's case, the Lord spoke to Daniel as he prayed and gave Daniel yet another vision, one filled with "seventy 'sevens'" (Dan. 9:24). *Seven* in the Hebrew language is a word that refers to fullness. Ten is a word in Hebrew that refers to the law and consequences associated with it. Seventy, therefore, was a word for the fullness of the law and its consequences, and to add "sevens" to that was to say, in effect, that this vision was about the fullness of the Law's fulfillment in all of its ultimately full effect! It was about the end of the end, the final of the final, the fulfillment of the fulfillment, the perfect fullness of the fullness.

What Daniel saw caused him such anxiety that he went into mourning, not eating, drinking, or bathing. The Lord sent an angel to give him understanding. When the angel spoke, Daniel bowed to the ground and couldn't speak.

Daniel saw what was durable, not fleeting.

Daniel saw what would happen in the end of the ages, not just what would happen at the end of seventy years.

Daniel saw what was God's vision for the whole of time, not merely a seventy-year period of Babylonian captivity.

Let me assure you, when God gives you a glimpse into the vision He has for your life and He lays it against the backdrop of eternity, you will be shocked at what you see. Life will take on a seriousness, a depth, and an importance that it has never had before. Decisions will be easier to make because you will have a full grasp of what is at stake—not only for a short time, but for all time. Choices you make will be clearer because you have a stronger understanding about who God has called you to be.

Ask God to give you a power-of-one vision for your life. You'll never be the same!

As Daniel was bowed to the ground, the angel said to him, "Do not be afraid, O man highly esteemed. . . . Peace! Be strong now; be strong" (Dan. 10:19).

"Fear not. Be strong and of good courage." You'll find those phrases in the Bible dozens of times. They are God's words to you right now. A power-of-one vision can be so awesome you feel fear. You can be paralyzed by the destiny God has for you. The Lord, however, does not want you to live in fear of making decisions. He wants you to face the future with peace and great courage.

From my own experience, when God communicated His vision for my life in asking me to birth a new congregation, I was mortified. The reasons are many but God's call on my life to discover the power of one was exhilarating at the same time.

Is it any coincidence that Jesus referred to the Holy Spirit as our "Comforter" and our "Helper"? A comforter gives encouragement and peace. A helper is one who gives us courage. Just to know such a helper is walking with us can make us feel invincible to the attacks of persecutors. Jesus wanted us to be assured that the Holy Spirit with us is the One who imparts peace and courage to us, and He will not abandon us as we walk in faith toward the fulfillment of the vision God has given us.

Trust the Holy Spirit today to lead you into the path of good choices and right decisions!

Establishing Christ's Presence in Your World

Write down in one sentence what you believe to be your primary purpose on this earth: who it is that God has created you to be and what it is that God has called you to do.

Write down a key decision or choice you are facing today.

Lay the two statements next to each other.

How is the statement about your life's vision related to the decision or choice you are facing right now?

Begin to write down all of the consequences or factors that you perceive to be related to this choice or decision. Identify any lasting consequences that may be associated with one choice over another. Identify how this decision impacts the fulfillment of your lifetime purpose.

Reflect or Discuss

- How difficult is it to maintain a long-range or lifetime perspective when you face immediate opportunities or choices that demand action right away?
- What strategies might you use to evaluate the big picture associated with a choice or decision?

Do today what will favorably impact tomorrow.

CHAPTER TWENTY-EIGHT

You Can Live Free of Worry

Worry is a form of fear.

It is a fear that things aren't going to turn out as you desire or expect.

It is a fear that you are going to be hurt or rejected in the future, or that something shameful from your past is going to come to light.

It is a fear that you will be found lacking or failing.

It is a fear that you won't be loved or counted as lovable.

It is a fear that God won't come through for you to protect you, provide for you, or nurture you as you desperately need or long for Him to do.

Worry is a major contributor to stress in our society today, and stress is rampant. As strong, righteous, and coura-

Do not be anxious about anything.
(PHILIPPIANS 4:6)

geous as Daniel appeared to be throughout his life, Daniel was also subject to fear, especially when he experienced visions from God that depicted future events that were overwhelmingly evil and devastatingly destructive.

The Bible says about the aftermath of one particular vision: "I, Daniel, mourned for three weeks. I ate no choice foods; no meat or wine touched my lips; and I used no lotions at all until the three weeks were over" (Dan. 10:2–3). Then, when the angel gave the vision's meaning to him, he "had no strength left, my face turned deathly pale, and I was helpless. . . . I fell into a deep sleep, my face to the ground" (Dan. 10:8–9).

The visions that caused such deep distress in Daniel were true, but they were not for the immediate future. They related to times in the far distant future. Even so, they filled him with dread.

At the time Daniel had these visions, he was in his eighties. One might think that an old man who had done it all and seen it all in his lifetime would not be subject to fear. Not so! No person, at any age or any degree of spiritual maturity, is immune to bouts of anxiety or fear. The challenge facing all of us is to know how to evaluate our worries and fears, and then how to overcome them.

To be an effective power-of-one Christian, you must be able to overcome anxiety and fear.

Evaluating Your Worries

People who have studied anxiety have concluded from their research studies that 40 percent of what we worry about never happens, 30 percent of what we worry about is in the past and we can't change anything about it, 12 percent of people worry needlessly about their health, 10 percent are petty and miscellaneous anxieties that will seem inconsequential in the near future, and 8 percent of the worries we have are "light worries" about which we can actually do something.

The word *worry* comes from a German word that means "to strangle." If we feel an anxiety, we need to evaluate it immediately.

Is it strangling us? Is it related to something we can do something about? If the answer is yes to either of these questions, we need immediately to go to prayer about the matter and then take positive action.

A scientist once determined that the dense fog that enveloped his city from time to time, if condensed, would amount to about one glass of water! Worry is like that. It is a state of mind that clouds our ability to see things accurately, at times paralyzing us from taking action. If what you are worrying about is in any way inhibiting you from completing your daily chores or responsibilities, that worry is unhealthy! Go to prayer, and take positive action.

Sometimes a person needs help in letting go of the past. If that's the case, get help. You need to address any worry that is rooted in sin, guilt, or shame. Go to God for forgiveness and ask Him to cleanse your mind of all thoughts and memories that may haunt you or cripple you emotionally.

Sometimes a person needs help in determining how best to address a worry or fear with positive action. If that's the case, get help! There are countless things a person can do to keep a negative situation from happening, or to keep from being shackled by a fear that God will not provide or protect sufficiently.

Jesus had this to say about worry:

Do not worry about your life, what you will eat or drink; or about your body, what you will wear. Is not life more important than food, and the body more important than clothes? Look at the birds of the air; they do not sow or reap or store away in barns, and yet your heavenly Father feeds them. Are you not much more valuable than they? Who of you by worrying can add a single hour to his life?

And why do you worry about clothes? See how the lilies of the field grow. They do not labor or spin. Yet I tell you that not even Solomon in all his splendor was dressed like one of these. If that is how God clothes the grass of the field, which is here today and tomorrow is thrown into the fire, will he not much more clothe you, O you of little faith? So do not worry, saying, "What shall we eat?" or "What shall we drink?" or "What shall we wear?" For the pagans run after all these things and your heavenly Father knows that you need them. But seek first the kingdom and his righteousness, and all these things will be given to you as well. Therefore do not worry about tomorrow, for tomorrow will worry about itself. Each day has enough trouble of its own. (Matthew 6:25–34)

Jesus' teaching had to do with priorities. When we are pursuing what is truly important in our lives, many of the little things pale in comparison. A person who is in a life-and-death struggle against a terrible disease often has little anxiety about whether the dry cleaner is going to get a spot out of a dress or if the postal service is going to deliver a birthday card on time. A person who truly is concerned about the big issues of life doesn't sweat the small stuff.

Take Charge of Your Thoughts

Worry is mental. To stop worrying you need to take charge of your thoughts. And how do you do that? You choose to think about something other than the topic that worries you! The apostle Paul gave two powerful truths:

First, turn your anxiety-laden thoughts to praise and prayer (Phil. 4:4, 6). Voice your praise to God. Begin to exalt Him as greater than whatever problem is facing you. Thank Him for resolving any worries you may have with His answers and His provision. Thank Him for taking on your enemies and defeating them.

Ask God very specifically for what you want to see happen, what you want to receive, or what you want to be allowed to do. Praise Him for making a good future not only possible, but inevitable!

Second, focus your thoughts on what is positive. Force yourself to focus and to think about what is "true . . . noble . . . right . . . pure . . . lovely . . . admirable." If there is any aspect of the situation facing you that is "excellent or praiseworthy," think about that! (Phil. 4:8).

Do What Works

"But," you may be saying, "it's so hard *not* to worry." If you have a long-standing habit of worrying, that may be true. But the good news is that you can change your thinking patterns. You can decide that you are going to turn from worry, which doesn't produce anything positive, to doing positive work, which has great potential for producing many things that are positive! Let me share three brief stories that may help you.

The first story is about a woman who was considering the possibility of starting her own business. She had lots of worries about whether her business would succeed. She confided her fears to her father. He wisely said to her, "What's the worst thing that can happen?"

"I can fail and lose my money."

"So," her father said, "you'll find a way to replace the money by doing something else."

"People will laugh at me," she said.

Her father replied, "Actually, they probably won't care."

"They won't?" she said, a little surprised at his answer.

"People usually care only about themselves," her father said. "When they see a group photo, they only see themselves, not the other people. When they go to a party, they are concerned more about what they are wearing, not what others have on. People rarely remember a month after an event who was there, what happened, or what was served—at least not fully or accurately."

"But I really want to succeed," the woman said.

"You will!" her father said. "You will succeed, if at nothing else, in learning whether you can or cannot make money in this business venture."

Her father then advised her to have her business plan checked out by somebody who had been successful in a business similar to hers. He advised her to really do her homework about all aspects of the business before she spent much money on inventory, rent, or advertising. He advised her to pray about God's best timing to launch the business, and to ask God to lead her to the very best location for opening her store.

The more this woman took to heart what her father had said, and the more she did her homework, the more she found herself so busy that she didn't have time to be worried or fearful! And yes, her business was a success.

The second story is about a man who was facing a firm deadline with a tremendous amount of work still to be done on the project facing him. He said, "I was really worried, and then I realized that I was spending more time worrying about the work ahead of me than doing it. I finally said, *I don't know if I can get all this done, but I also don't know that I can't get it all done, so I have to try.*" He put all of his efforts into the doing and none of his energy into the worrying. And yes, he met the deadline.

The third story is about a little girl who was worried about her first day of school. "What if nobody at school likes me?" she said to her mother.

"Like yourself!" her mother said.

The little girl giggled, but her mother was serious. "If you like yourself, other people will be attracted to you and like you too. If you are stressed out about how you look or how you should act, other people will feel that stress and they'll walk away. Take the attitude that you are going to do your best, look your best, and be friendly. Trust me, honey, the teacher and the other children are going to like you!"

Her mother was right.

What are the lessons here for the person who desires to exert power-of-one influence?

Prepare yourself as best you know how for a successful outcome and a successful life. Do what you know to do. Then trust God to do what only God can do.

Stay focused. Don't procrastinate. Keep working. Keep your mind occupied with what you can do and what is happening, not with what you can't do and what might or might not happen.

Stay positive. Remind yourself that God owns everything, controls everything, and provides everything we need—we need to do only what is most important in God's eyes and then trust Him to meet our needs. Choose to believe that He will make a way for you to succeed even if there doesn't seem to be a way.

Focus on the Tasks Required

God did not give visions to Daniel for him to worry about them. He gave Daniel visions so he would write them down and pass them on to future generations. God trusted Daniel to "write it right" for those who would follow. In the end, the messenger from God said to Daniel, "As for you, go your way till the end. You will rest, and then at the end of the days you will rise to receive your allotted inheritance" (Dan. 12:13).

What a wonderful word this is to us if we are prone to worry and fear! God says, "Live out your life to the best of your ability. Trust God to the best of your faith. Leave the consequences to Him!"

Establishing Christ's Presence in Your World
Write down three things you are worried about.

Next to each item, write down two positive things you can do *right now*—and if not today, then tomorrow morning or in the very near future—to counteract any negative consequences you fear.

Then, do those things!

Reflect or Discuss

- How difficult is it to change a habitual way of thinking?
- What might a person do to "take captive" every negative thought and replace it with a positive one (2 Cor. 10:5)?

Focus on today. Be mindful of the good around you, and work to make things even better.

CHAPTER TWENTY-NINE

You Can Entrust the Dangerous Situation to Christ

The visions Daniel had about the end of time were almost beyond description. They filled this normally courageous man with dread. He said to the messenger from God who came to help him and inform him further, "I am overcome with anguish because of the vision, my lord, and I am helpless. How can I, your servant, talk with you, my lord? My strength is gone and I can hardly breathe" (Dan. 10:16–17).

Have you ever felt so overwhelmed by a situation facing you, or someone you love, that you were filled with anguish?

Have you ever felt utterly helpless?

Have you ever felt so weak that you didn't know how you could take another breath, much less talk?

Sacrifice thank offerings to God,

fulfill your vows to the Most High,

and call upon me in the day of trouble;

I will deliver you, and you will honor me.

(PSALM 50:14–15)

That's the way Daniel felt.

You may not have been given a vision of the end of times, but you may have been given news that made you face squarely the possibility of the end of "a time." Perhaps the news is related to the end of your time on this earth. Perhaps it was news about the end of your time in a relationship, in a business or a career, or in a home you love.

The doctor may have announced to you a feared diagnosis, with the added words "There's really nothing we can do at this stage—go home and get your affairs in order."

The call may have come in the middle of the night to tell you that your child is missing—and it appears that a crime may be involved.

The raging storm may be bearing down on your loved ones, who don't know there's a storm coming and have made no preparations to escape it.

The financial report may signal the end game for your business.

The coach may tell you that your contract is not being renewed and it's time to hang up your athletic career.

The planning commission may have reached a final decision that requires you to move out of your home.

Your spouse may tell you, with bags packed and loaded in the car, that your marriage is hopelessly dead and there's another person awaiting across town.

The plane may be going down, the ship may be sinking, the murderous terrorists may have taken control—figuratively if not literally.

What can and should you do?

Everything in you wants to make a difference.

Everything in you wants to turn things around.

Everything in you wants to wake up and have the nightmare be over.

There are countless situations in life in which a person deeply desires to unleash his or her personal power of one but has no ability, no opportunity, or no understanding about what he or she might do.

That's the position in which Daniel found himself. Daniel was a can-do man. He had decades of successful accomplishments behind him. But as he faced a vivid description of the coming days, he also faced the stark reality that there was absolutely nothing he could do about the coming horror.

He trembled on his hands and knees.

The Command to Rise

Daniel wrote, "I had no strength left, my face was turned deathly pale and I was helpless. Then I heard him speaking, and as I listened to him, I fell into a deep sleep, my face to the ground." Then the messenger from the Lord said to Daniel, "Stand up, for I have now been sent to you" (Dan. 10:8–9, 11). And Daniel stood up.

The two most important words you may ever hear as you face a deeply troubling crisis are these: stand up! Everything in you may be crying out, "I can't." God says, "You can. Get up."

In the physical world, you may not be able to stand up. But on the inside—in your soul and in your spirit—you can rise up. If you can hear and comprehend the words "stand up," then you can stand up in your innermost being. Not only can you do it, you must do it.

"But I don't want to do it," you may moan. You may want the draperies to stay tightly shut, the door to stay locked, and for people to go away. You may want to sleep and not wake up. Denial and depression often manifest themselves in endless hours of sleep.

God says, "Stand up."

You may want to run away and hide. You may want to ignore the reality and continue on as if nothing has been said.

God says, "Face it."

You may see absolutely no point in taking any action, wash your hands of the entire problem, and proclaim yourself detached from any responsibility for the problem.

God says, "Deal with it."

You may find yourself wringing your hands, perplexed, not knowing what to do first.

God says, "I'll show you what I want you to understand, what I want you to do, and how I want you to respond."

God confronts us in our weakness and lack of faith. Jesus said repeatedly to His disciples, "Oh you of little faith!" "Where's your faith?" "Get with it—use your faith!" He said repeatedly to those He healed or delivered, "Get up. Get moving. Change your ways, stop sinning, and get on with your life."

God comforts and God counsels and God encourages the discouraged heart. In many cases, God also confronts and challenges and convicts. He doesn't leave us in our sin, He doesn't leave us in despair, He doesn't leave us puzzled. If we truly want His answers and His help, He will give them. The Lord gives you the ability to have power-of-one influence—He wants you to succeed in using that ability!

A New Understanding

The Lord did not reveal, perhaps, the whole of the reason He gave end-time visions to Daniel, but the messenger of the Lord did reveal the part of the reason that Daniel needed to know.

When you are facing a dire situation or a perplexing dilemma that drives you into fear, you need to learn what God desires to teach you in that hour. He may not tell you everything you want to know, but He will tell you everything He wants you to learn if you will ask Him to instruct you.

The Lord may not tell you what will happen to another person or group, but He will reveal to you what you need to know in order for His purposes to be accomplished in you and through you.

The Lord's lesson may be one of repentance—the Lord may be calling you to leave behind a particular sin and move into greater righteousness.

His lesson may be one of trust—the Lord may be allowing this situation so that you will turn from something that you have come to trust or love as much as or more than you love the Lord.

His lesson may be one of insight—the Lord may desire to give you greater insight into His plans and purposes so that you can teach and prepare others around you.

His lesson may be one of witness—the Lord may be allowing this situation in your life so that you can show, by your words and deeds, what it truly means to be a Christian.

His lesson may be one of preparation—the Lord may be calling you to leave some things so you can open your hands and heart to receive other things He wants you to have. He may be calling you to leave one place so He can direct you to another greater place of ministry or effectiveness. He may be calling you to become prepared so you are capable of handling the greater blessing He desires to give you.

One thing we can always count on is that God uses difficult times to refine us and test us. He will use persecution and difficulty to deepen our dependency upon Him and mold us more completely into the full character of Christ Jesus. The more we depend on Him, and the more we become like Jesus, the more power-of-one authority and influence the Lord entrusts to us.

The Lord addressed a time of persecution by saying through the prophet Zechariah that He would bring His people

> into the fire;
>   I will refine them like silver
>   and test them like gold.
> They will call on my name
>   and I will answer them.
> I will say, "They are my people,"
>   and they will say, "The LORD is our God."
> (ZECHARIAH 13:9)

The refining fires of the Lord can seem exceedingly hot to us at times, but the end result is always exceedingly beautiful to the Lord—*if* we will submit to what the Lord is doing and call upon Him. Suffering and persecution do not automatically produce godly behavior. In some cases they produce bitterness and anger, yet that is not what happened to the apostle Paul. That is why he concluded in Romans 8:39 that nothing would succeed in separating him from the love of God.

It is those who turn to the Lord in times of suffering and persecution who experience the Lord's work in their innermost beings. They are the ones who grow lovelier even as their bodies become sicker, the ones whose witness shines brighter even as they become weaker, the ones who have a peace that passes all understanding even as the tumult around them grows more chaotic.

The first purpose of God's giving His visions to Daniel was so that Daniel would pass along the visions to instruct God's people about what was happening as the terrible and fearful events unfolded before them. God wanted his people to have understanding.

What the Righteous Are Called to Do

The Lord's messenger gave insights to Daniel that also indicated what would happen to the righteous people during the horrible days to come. The words of this messenger gave insight into how God's people were to respond as a powerful leader arose and wreaked havoc on all he came to rule. The word of the Lord to Daniel was this:

> The people who know their God will firmly resist him. Those who are wise will instruct many, though for a time they will fall by the sword or be burned or captured or plundered. When they fall, they will receive a little help, and many who are not sincere will join them. Some of the wise will stumble, so that they may be refined, purified and made spotless until the time of the end. (Daniel 11:32–35)

I do not know with certainty that we are living in this time that Daniel foresaw, but I think that's a great possibility. I do know that we live in a violent and treacherous world, with racial groups in escalating conflict, tribal groups and nations at war, families being torn apart, and churches and denominations undergoing deep division. I do know that we live in a world in which black is called white, when morality has been turned upside down, and when people are feeling as if they have been turned inside out with confusion, stress, and uncertainty about what to believe and whom to trust. The devil's lies and schemes, although not new, have become increasingly subtle and manipulative. The motives of even godly people are increasingly unclear, while the actions of even the most ungodly people are increasingly tolerated.

God's desire is that we wake up and then stand up!

Hallmarks of Righteous People

The Lord gave Daniel five hallmarks of the righteous people who would encounter the evil dictator of the world and the devil who manipulated him. The behaviors required of them are the same ones required of us.

1. RESIST THE DEVIL

We are called to be a people who will resist the temptations and deceitful actions of the devil. God's promise to us is: "Resist the devil, and he will flee from you" (James 4:7).

2. RESIST EVIL PEOPLE AND THEIR DICTATES

We are called to be a people who will resist the orders of evil men and women. The Bible tells us clearly: "You adulterous people, don't you know that friendship with the world is hatred toward God? Anyone who chooses to be a friend of the world becomes an enemy of God" (James 4:4).

3. CONTINUE IN FAITH

We are called to be a people who will remain constant in our faith and good works, even though we may be persecuted or our ranks may be infiltrated with the unfaithful. The Lord challenges us: "Be patient ... until the Lord's coming. See how the farmer waits for the land to yield its valuable crop and how patient he is for the autumn and spring rains. You too, be patient and stand firm, because the Lord's coming is near" (James 5:7–8).

4. CONTINUE TO INSTRUCT OTHERS IN RIGHTEOUSNESS

We are never called to cower in silence. Rather, we are called to continue to "instruct many." If we know what to do, if we know what is right, if we know the truth, we are called to communicate what we know to others. Many times that communication is not in words, but in the deeds of our lives. God's Word challenges us: "Who is wise and understanding among you? Let him show it by his good life, by deeds done in the humility that comes from wisdom" (James 3:13).

5. SUBMIT TO GOD

We are called to submit to God's plan for us, which is to refine and cleanse us until the day when we are completely without blemish before Him. The Bible challenges us: "Come near to God and he will come near to you. Wash your hands, you sinners, and purify your hearts, you double-minded. . . . Humble yourselves before the Lord, and he will lift you up" (James 4:8, 10).

The Prerequisites for God's Help

God's pledge to us throughout His Word is that if we will resist the devil and those in whom the devil is at work, and submit completely to God—praising Him and obeying Him—He will deliver us from evil. Let's take a closer look at the verses with which this chapter begins.

SACRIFICE THANK OFFERINGS TO GOD

In a time of great anguish, don't stop thanking the Lord for His goodness toward you. Don't stop praising His name. In times of anguish, perhaps more than any other time, giving thanks and praise are truly sacrificial. A sacrifice of thanksgiving and praise costs something, it is hard to do, but God requires it nonetheless.

Thank and praise the Lord as long as it takes for you to feel a renewal in your heart and to experience the strength that comes from deep praise. Thank and praise the Lord throughout the day and throughout the night. Any time you awaken in fear or are gripped by doubt, begin to thank and praise the Lord.

FULFILL YOUR VOWS TO THE MOST HIGH

To "fulfill your vows" is to continue to keep God's commandments. It is to obey the Lord and to continue to acknowledge Him as your Savior and to follow Him as your Lord. In other words, renew your commitment to the Lord.

CALL UPON THE LORD IN THE DAY OF TROUBLE

Cry out to the Lord in complete dependence upon Him. Trust Him as never before with your whole heart and every aspect of your life.

God's promise to you is that if you will do these things, He will deliver you. He may not deliver you as you desire to be delivered. He may heal through death, not in life. He may restore you by placing you in new situations and among new people, not in changing the old situation or changing the hearts of the people who presently surround you. He may deliver you by taking you out of the place where you are and putting you in a greater place of His choosing and design. Trust God to know how, when, with whom, and for what purposes He delivers you.

A life of complete obedience and submission to God is a life that brings honor to Him — and in that, your reward will be great.

Establishing Christ's Presence in Your World

Write down the greatest problem you are facing today. Ask the Lord to show you what He desires you to understand about that problem. Ask Him to show you how He wants you to respond to the problem. Write down those insights next to the problem you have cited.

Begin to write down a list of things for which you are thankful. Write down a list of praises to the Lord. When you feel overwhelmed with fear, anguish, sorrow, or confusion, get out your list and even if you don't feel like thanking and praising the Lord, begin to voice that list aloud to the Lord. As you think of new things to add to each list, do so!

Identify a very specific way in which you feel you need to express greater submission to the Lord. In what area of your life do you need to trust God with a greater trust or yield the decision-making power to Him more completely?

Are there concrete steps you can take that will reflect a greater degree of submission?

Reflect or Discuss

- Submission to the Lord in a time of difficulty is ultimately a matter of pride. How difficult is it to admit to the Lord, yourself, and even to others that you cannot solve a particular problem, resolve a particular disagreement, or reconcile a particular relationship? How difficult is it to come to the place where you accept the fact that although God can solve, resolve, or bring about reconciliation, He may choose not to do so for the greater and eternal good of both you and others involved? How difficult is it to lay down the prideful attitude of trying to dictate to God how and when He should act?

God knows what you do not know. Trust Him to tell you what you need to know.

CHAPTER THIRTY

You Can Entrust the Unpredictable Outcome to Our Faithful God

There are times when God is silent. He does not tell us what we want to know, or what we think we need to know.

We need to grow in our faith so we might discern whether God is choosing to remain silent, or we just aren't listening closely enough.

There are times when God calls us to be silent. He does not authorize us to speak or act, but rather to stand still.

We need to grow in our faith so we might discern when we are to act, and when we are to refrain from acting.

It can take just as much courage to stand still as it takes to march boldly into the fray of battle. It takes great faith to continue to trust God when He remains

Since ancient times no one has heard,
no ear has perceived,
no eye has seen any God besides you,
who acts on behalf of those who wait for him.

(ISAIAH 64:4)

totally silent about an issue, relationship, environment, or situation that is troublesome to us.

Daniel was given a powerful vision of the end and he said to the messenger who came to inform him about his vision, "I heard, but I did not understand. So I asked, 'My lord, what will the outcome of all this be?'" (Dan. 12:8).

Isn't that the very question that is often on our lips?

How will this turn out?

What will happen to me, my family or loved ones, or to all of us?

Who will still be standing when the storm has passed?

Will we live or die?

The messenger of the Lord said to Daniel, "Go your way, Daniel, because the words are closed up and sealed until the time of the end" (Dan. 12:9).

Daniel was told in part. He was not told the whole.

"I Know Who Knows"

A person once said to me, "I am very frustrated."

"Why?" I asked.

"I just attended a school board meeting. A group of us parents have become concerned at falling test scores at the school and we met with the principal about two weeks ago. He told us on the one hand, the population in our area is changing and the new kids in the school are behind. On the other hand, he said the parents weren't requiring their children to do their homework, but he had little authority to make the parents and children comply with homework assignments. Then on the other hand, he said some students needed tutors or remedial instruction. But on the other hand, he said there wasn't enough money in the budget for tutors or remedial instruction. When he got to about the sixth or seventh 'other hand,' one of the parents asked him if he had any ideas about solutions that might work. He said, 'No, not really.'"

"That's when you decided to go to the school board?" I asked.

"Yes," she said. "The board members talked for more than an hour and the bottom line was, *nobody* knows what to do even though everybody agrees something should be done. I came away from that meeting wondering if I should homeschool my children or try to put them in a private school or hire a tutor. 'Not knowing' seems to be catching, and it is very frustrating not to know what to do or what the consequences might be!"

Everything about her face and tone of voice assured me that she really was frustrated. We often find ourselves frustrated at "not knowing."

Daniel may have been frustrated too.

Without falling into the mode this principal had adopted . . . On the one hand we are quick to say that we don't want God to reveal to us what will happen in our lives in the next five years—at least not the whole of what will happen. We don't want to know the sadness and difficulties that may lie ahead.

On the other hand, we are a society that is quick to read the daily horoscope in the morning paper as if it's a reliable clue to what will happen during the day. We are eager to know who will win, who will lose, how things will turn out, and what the market will do. The vast majority of any news program and news talk show—on radio or television—does not deal with facts exclusively. There's a tremendous amount of speculation about what might happen, what should happen, and who could be the key players that will be involved.

We are conflicted in our desire to know and not know.

God makes it plain in His Word that there are many things we cannot know because we have finite minds. There are other things that we are not to know because such knowledge might devastate us or put us in greater danger. At times we are called simply to let God be the only One who knows.

A wise person said to me not long ago about a very serious problem she was facing, "I don't know what will happen. But I know who knows! I'm holding on to His hand very tightly."

That's the best position we can be in! Knowing God means

knowing that God knows! And trusting God means trusting God with every detail of an outcome.

One of the greatest statements the Lord makes in His Word about His omnipotence—His sovereign power over all things—and about His omniscience—His all-encompassing knowledge and wisdom—is found in the book of Job. The Lord spoke to Job in the midst of a blinding blizzard. Among the many questions God asked Job were these:

Where were you when I laid the earth's foundation?
(JOB 38:4)

Have you ever given orders to the morning,
　or shown the dawn its place?
(JOB 38:12)

Have you journeyed to the springs of the sea
　or walked in the recesses of the deep?
. . . Have you seen the gates of the shadow of death?
Have you comprehended the vast expanses of the earth?
(JOB 38:16–18)

Do you know when the mountain goats give birth?
(JOB 39:1)

Will the wild ox consent to serve you?
(JOB 39:9)

Does the eagle soar at your command?
(JOB 39:27)

The answers, of course, to all of these questions were and are "No." God's wisdom and power are unlimited. Man's abilities to comprehend and remember are all very limited. The apostle Paul wrote that this is true even about spiritual matters in our own lives:

"Now we see but a poor reflection as in a mirror; then we shall see face to face. Now I know in part; then I shall know fully, even as I am fully known" (1 Cor. 13:12).

We do not fully know ourselves.

We certainly cannot fully know another person.

We do not know fully what we will be doing twenty-four hours from now.

We certainly cannot know what we will be doing five, ten, or twenty years from now.

But God knows.

And we can know Him.

Obstacles to Our Trust

We face two great challenges when it comes to entrusting the unknown and the mysterious to God. These challenges are polar opposites.

1. THE OBSTACLE OF PRIDE

The first challenge we face in trusting God with the future is our own pride. We want to think we are in control of our own lives and therefore, we can make plans and set goals and determine our own destiny. Hundreds of books are available in the bookstores of our nation today that have that premise at their core: "You can be the success you want to be!"

God's Word tells us,

> Now listen, you who say, "Today or tomorrow we will go to this or that city, spend a year there, carry on business and make money." Why, you do not even know what will happen tomorrow. What is your life? You are a mist that appears for a little while and then vanishes. Instead, you ought to say, "If it is the Lord's will, we will live and do this or that." As it is, you boast and brag. All such boasting is evil. (James 4:13–16)

I'm certainly not against making plans or setting goals. We need to be very careful in all of our goal-setting, however. We must always recognize that we know only in part what God is calling us to do. We must make certain that we desire above all else that His plans and purposes be accomplished in us and through us.

We do nothing in our own strength or ability—we are capable of succeeding only to the degree that He allows us to work, create, and minister. He sets the boundaries for our behavior. He establishes the ceiling of our success. He governs the degree to which we can gain understanding about any particular issue or problem.

2. THE OBSTACLE OF LAZINESS

At the other end of the spectrum, we find those who take the position: "Well, if God wants it done, He'll do it. If God wants me to know that, He'll drop that knowledge into my mind. If God wants me to undertake a task and succeed at it, He'll drop all of the resources I need right into my lap." God invites us to a partnership in accomplishing things on this earth, with God as the Producer, Director, Enabler, Provider, and Protector, and Source of all things. Our part is to trust and to do the work He puts before us to do.

If we fail to trust, we fail.

If we fail to work, we fail.

The Word of God challenges us, "Faith by itself, if it is not accompanied by action, is dead" (James 2:17).

Sometimes the work God gives us to do is sheer practice, practice, practice. The gifts and talents God gives us come to us in an embryonic state. We must grow our gifts into maturity. We must practice our skills to perfection.

Sometimes the work God gives us is repetitive. It can feel like drudgery. God promised Abraham a land, but then He commanded him to walk it out—to cover it by the slowest and most tedious method possible: one foot up and one foot down (Gen. 13:17).

Sometimes the work God gives us is not at all what we would choose to do with our time, talents, or resources. We may not want to sit for hours by the side of a beloved one who is bedridden. We may not like going to the county jail to share the gospel with the prisoners there. We may not enjoy spending our vacation days working in a ghetto to help people who don't appear to want our help.

Sometimes the work God gives us seems menial, without any eternal purpose. The truth is, we never fully know who is watching us, who is listening to us, or who is being impacted by our faithfulness in doing the "small things." The Lord's promise to us is that those who are faithful in little are going to be given much responsibility down the line (Matt. 25:23).

The chores of this world are our responsibility as God places them in front of us to do. Don't shirk work. Don't slough off. Give your very best effort to the tasks God has entrusted to you. The power of one is not reserved for grand and noble gestures or high stages before large audiences. Power-of-one influence happens moment by moment, often as we do small and ordinary tasks.

A Balance of Knowing and Trusting

One area in which pride and laziness often collide is the degree to which we seek to know and understand God's Word and God's plans and purposes. Some people take the position: "I don't know and I don't want to know." Others take the position: "I've got to know and God's got to tell me." The balance between these positions is this: Study. Learn. Apply.

Immerse yourself in the whole of the Word of God. Don't just read the parts of God's Word that you find exciting or comforting. Read the parts that are challenging and convicting! If you don't understand what a passage means, study it until you have insight into the meaning. Ask someone who knows. Read and do research on the matter.

The more you know, the more you need to know how to apply what you learn. There's little usefulness in having a mind filled with knowledge that is never put to good use! Just knowing something is of little use unless you do something with that knowledge to bless others.

God's Word challenges us: "Do your best to present yourself to God as one approved, a workman who does not need to be ashamed and who correctly handles the word of truth" (2 Tim. 2:15).

The more you know, the more you are also likely to have questions and to come face-to-face with what you do not know. Those of us who have completed doctoral studies know that the end goal for a doctoral program—from the perspective of the professors, not necessarily the student—is to bring a student to the place where he admits he has more questions than answers. The intelligence of the questions that the student is still asking is far more important in a doctoral defense than the intelligence of the work he has already done. When a person is aware that he still has a great deal to learn, and yet is equipped with key information and an ability to conduct research, that person is deemed capable of going out into the world to find answers and to impart knowledge. Degree granted!

How important it is that we have this same perspective when it comes to knowing and applying the Word of God! We are to know all we can about God's Word. We are to apply it in the best and most noble ways we can. We are to continue to study and learn. We are to teach others what we know and challenge them to go beyond us in what they learn and do.

In the End . . .

Ultimately, the full outcome of what will happen in our lives, or as the result of our lives, is something we cannot know. Only God knows the fullness of the legacy we will leave behind. Only God knows how He will use our lives to impact the fullness of His plan for the ages. We cannot know, and we do not need to know. We need to study, work, and walk hour by hour and day by day as the Holy Spirit leads us.

Daniel did not need to know how the end of the age would turn out.

He only needed to know that God was in control, that God was

100 percent responsible, and that he and God were in close relationship.

That's all you need to know too.

Establishing Christ's Presence in Your World

What are the biggest questions you have about God, about your life's purpose, or about a situation you are facing? Write down several of those questions. Carefully evaluate each one. What might you study or do in order to gain answers? What task or work might you undertake as a way of getting answers?

Get together with others in your church or community to ask, "What are the biggest questions we have before us?" (Recognize that every goal or problem can be reduced to a set of questions that need to be answered.) Write down the key questions. What needs to be researched or done in order to get the right answers?

Get busy and do those things.

Reflect or Discuss

- How can a person put himself into position to discern God's plans for tomorrow? Next week? Next month? Next year?
- Is it important to discern overall direction before we discern the details? Or is it more important to trust God with each step and discern the overall direction over time?
- What are the main questions every person should ask about his eternal destiny?

To get the right answers, ask the right questions. To get the job done, work.

CHAPTER THIRTY-ONE

You Can Have a Glimpse of the Good End God Has Already Authorized

Daniel may not have received all of the information he desired. He may not have known the fullness of what God was entrusting to him in the visions about the end times. He may not have had all his questions answered as he desired to have them answered. Even so, Daniel received a glimpse into what can only be described as a great and glorious end: "Those who are wise will shine like the brightness of the heavens, and those who lead many to righteousness, like the stars for ever and ever" (Dan. 12:3).

The messenger of the Lord also said: "Many will be purified, made spotless and refined, but the wicked will continue to be wicked. None of the wicked

Now the dwelling of God is with men, and he will live with them. They will be his people, and God himself will be with them and be their God. He will wipe every tear from their eyes. There will be no more death or mourning or crying or pain, for the old order of things has passed away.
(REVELATION 21:3–4)

will understand, but those who are wise will understand" (Dan. 12:10).

You may not have all the answers you need. You may not fully understand all that God has done, is doing, or will do in your life or through your life to others. But the Lord has given you, as His beloved child and as a believer in His Son, Jesus Christ, a glimpse of your great and glorious end. Any time you may become discouraged about the world around you, about your failure to make changes that you perceive to be significant, or about the quickness with which time passes, read the last two chapters of the book of Revelation.

We win in the end! It is only in eternity that you will fully know all that you have done as a power-of-one Christian. Only in eternity will you be fully rewarded for your influence and faithfulness in standing against evil and for good. Nobody can predict the full extent of his or her reward. But oh, the rewards we do know about in our heavenly home! The Bible tells us about heaven:

- There is no night or death, nor pain or sorrow.
- Satan disappears forever.
- Nothing impure touches the people of God.
- The righteous walk in a free and full relationship with God, just as Adam and Eve walked with God before they disobeyed God.
- Life is eternal.
- Every need is fully provided for.
- The beauty of holiness and the beauty of heaven become one and the same.

As important as it is to do our utmost to stem the tide of evil in our world—to reverse bad laws, to turn around the immorality and amorality that are so pervasive in our culture, to restore dignity to human beings of all races, to reestablish the value of marriage and family, and to meet the needs of suffering humanity—the two most important things in your life and in the life of every other person are:

Accept Jesus Christ.

Encourage others to accept Jesus Christ.

Nothing else ultimately matters. The foremost reason for doing all of the things I just mentioned—reversing bad laws, reestablishing morality, working for racial justice, upholding marriage and family, and meeting the needs of those who are suffering and dying—is so we might have a greater opportunity and a stronger platform on which to proclaim the gospel of Jesus Christ. It is so we might have a peaceful environment in which to teach the commandments of God and make disciples of all nations. It is so we might have as much opportunity as possible to help people become whole spiritually, emotionally, and physically—fully prepared to spend eternity with our loving heavenly Father.

Your destiny as a Christian is to spend eternity declaring with other believers through the ages and from every kindred, tongue, and tribe that the Lord Jesus Christ, according to Revelation 5:12, is worthy to receive

- Power
- Wealth
- Wisdom
- Strength
- Honor
- Glory
- Praise.

Why have I listed these in a way that you can reference easily? Because these are the very things that the Lord also has for you in eternity, in a supply that would be mind-boggling to you if you could even begin to grasp one fraction of the fullness of these treasures prepared for you!

As you ascribe to the Lord, with the voices of the angels and all living creatures, these things the Lord is worthy to receive, He, in turn, will reward you with this same inheritance. How do we know this? God's Word tells us so:

> You received the Spirit of sonship. And by him we cry, "*Abba*, Father." The Spirit himself testifies with our spirit that we are God's children. Now if we are children, then we are heirs—heirs of God and co-heirs with Christ, if indeed we share in his sufferings in order that we may also share in his glory. (Romans 8:15–17)

Your heavenly future is one in which you will receive

- Great power and authority—to rule, govern, and accomplish tasks that are beyond your current imagination.
- Unlimited wealth and resources to accomplish anything the Lord directs you to do.
- Complete wisdom to understand all things fully that are related to what the Lord desires for you to accomplish in eternity.
- Perfect health and unlimited endurance.
- Honor and reward for not only who you are and what you have done in obeying the Lord on this earth, but honor and reward for all that you will do in obedience to the Lord for all eternity.
- Glory—beauty, bliss, majesty, and splendor beyond anything this earth can offer.
- Praise—appreciation, value, and recognition from the Lord Himself!

That's heaven!
That's your future life!
That's your eternal destiny!
Too often we depict heaven as a place where we will sit idly on clouds strumming harps and singing praise choruses. I certainly see nothing wrong with a little of that—I like music, singing, and the

idea of sitting on a cloud. But that isn't the sum total of what awaits us. Heaven is going to be a place of activity and relationships that are all marked by purity, purpose, and joyful pleasure.

But . . . only for those who truly receive Jesus Christ as Savior and love and serve Jesus Christ as Lord.

The glorious end that awaits us is worth any amount of struggle we may face today.

Struggle is temporary.

Glory is forever.

Live today so that you can live all the tomorrows God desires for you to experience in His presence.

Establishing Christ's Presence in Your World

What is the one thing that you would most like to help change or influence in your world today? In what way does your desire include the winning of souls and the discipleship of those who believe in Jesus? Place your plans and goals against the template of eternity: What becomes unnecessary? What becomes vital?

To what people is the Holy Spirit leading you to talk about accepting Jesus or becoming more serious about their walks with the Lord? Make an appointment. Do it now.

Reflect or Discuss

- How easy is it to get so caught up in the problems and challenges of today that we lose sight of eternity?
- In what ways can we stay more mindful of the eternity that awaits those who trust in Jesus Christ?

Commit today: I may just be one person, but I can trust an awesome God to do His singular and holy work in me and through me—and that will make all the difference necessary for me to experience a great and glorious end.